Color Me Scared!
Halloween Adult Coloring Book

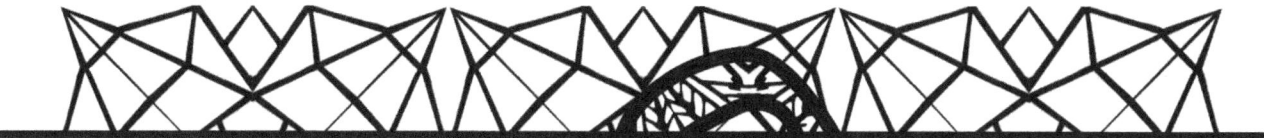

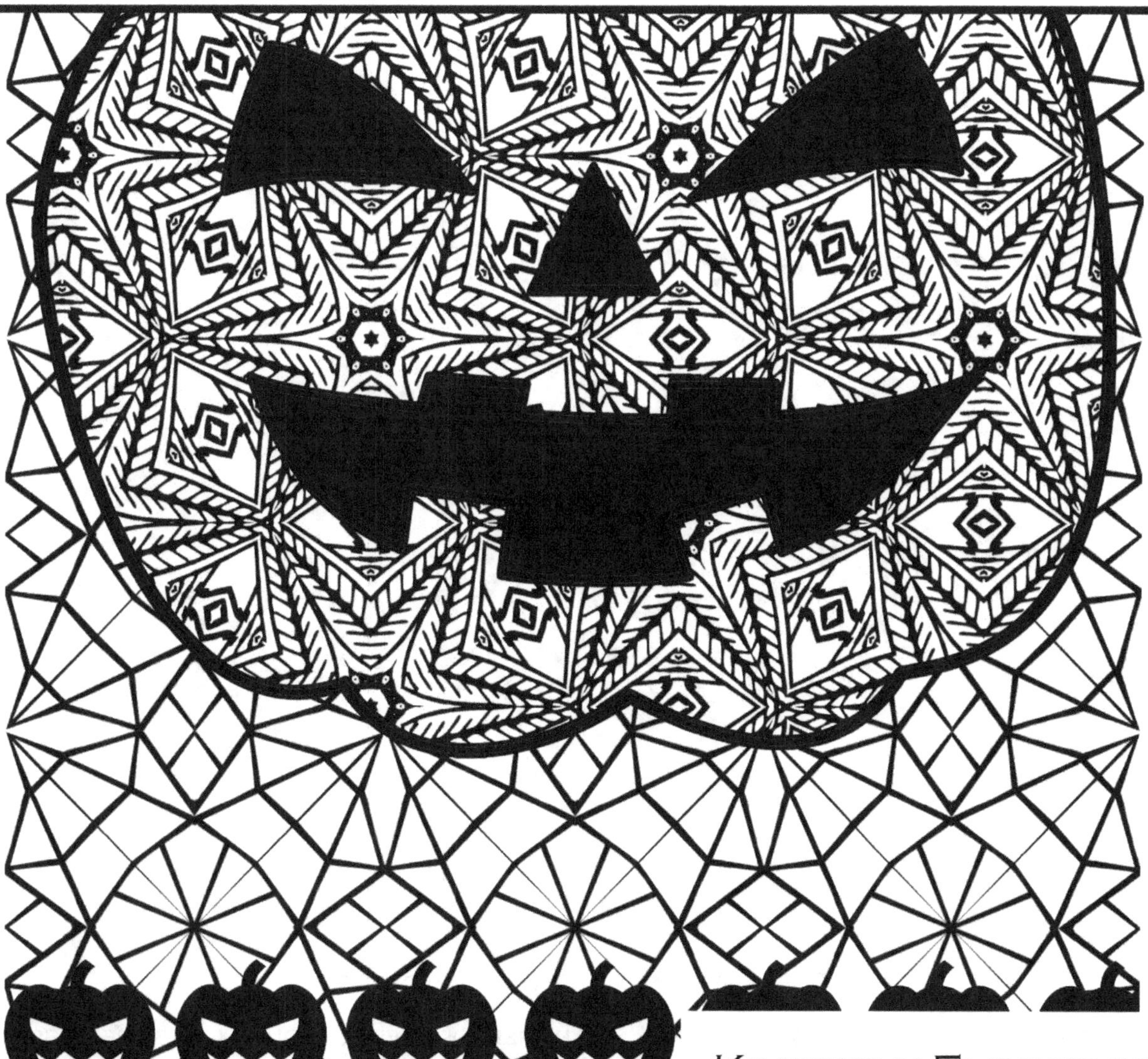

Kimberly Eldredge

Copyright © 2017 Kimberly Eldredge

Images are for personal use only and may not be reproduced without express permission of the author.

All rights reserved.

ISBN: 1979282765
ISBN-13: 978-1979282765

For Connor

ABOUT THIS BOOK

Do you remember stretching out on the floor, box of crayons or markers at your elbow, coloring your way through dozens of cartoon illustrations? You weren't trying to create art, you were just coloring…

Maybe time even seemed to pause while you were coloring. Or you'd only stop when you got uncomfortable from laying on the floor.

Coloring was fun. There was no right or wrong color; no right answer to how you were choosing to fill in your coloring book. And then, somewhere in the growing up process, doing something for fun, where the biggest decision was which shade of green and how hard to press, got lost. Life became all about tests and grades and dating… Then you grew up some more and life became about bills, money, promotions, housework, cooking, bosses, and stress.

While this coloring book can't fix the fact that you're not Peter Pan, it can help you regain that gentle fun of a fresh box of crayons and a brand new coloring book.

So go ahead, pull out that fresh-from-the-box crayon and enjoy! There's no right, no wrong, just patterns for you to enjoy!

HOW TO USE THIS BOOK

Isn't it a rather sad commentary that you need to have a "how to use this book" section for a coloring book? Here's the deal:
COLOR.
Don't worry about 'right' or 'wrong' or if you're doing it the same was your best friend is or the way the lady in Hootenanny Holler is doing it! (By the way, that's a real place!)
So break out the markers or colored pencils. Steal the crayons from your kid. Add in glitter or ribbon or whatever! It's up to you! It's not about creating a masterpiece, it's about recapturing that feeling of enjoying watching the colors slide onto the pages, hearing the soft scratch of the crayon or pencil across the page, getting bright colors on your hands and not caring.
If you want to get really technical with it, yes, you can cut the pages out. Or slide a blank piece of copy paper between the pages in case the markers bleed through.
Just do yourself one huge favor:

ENJOY COLORING IN IT!

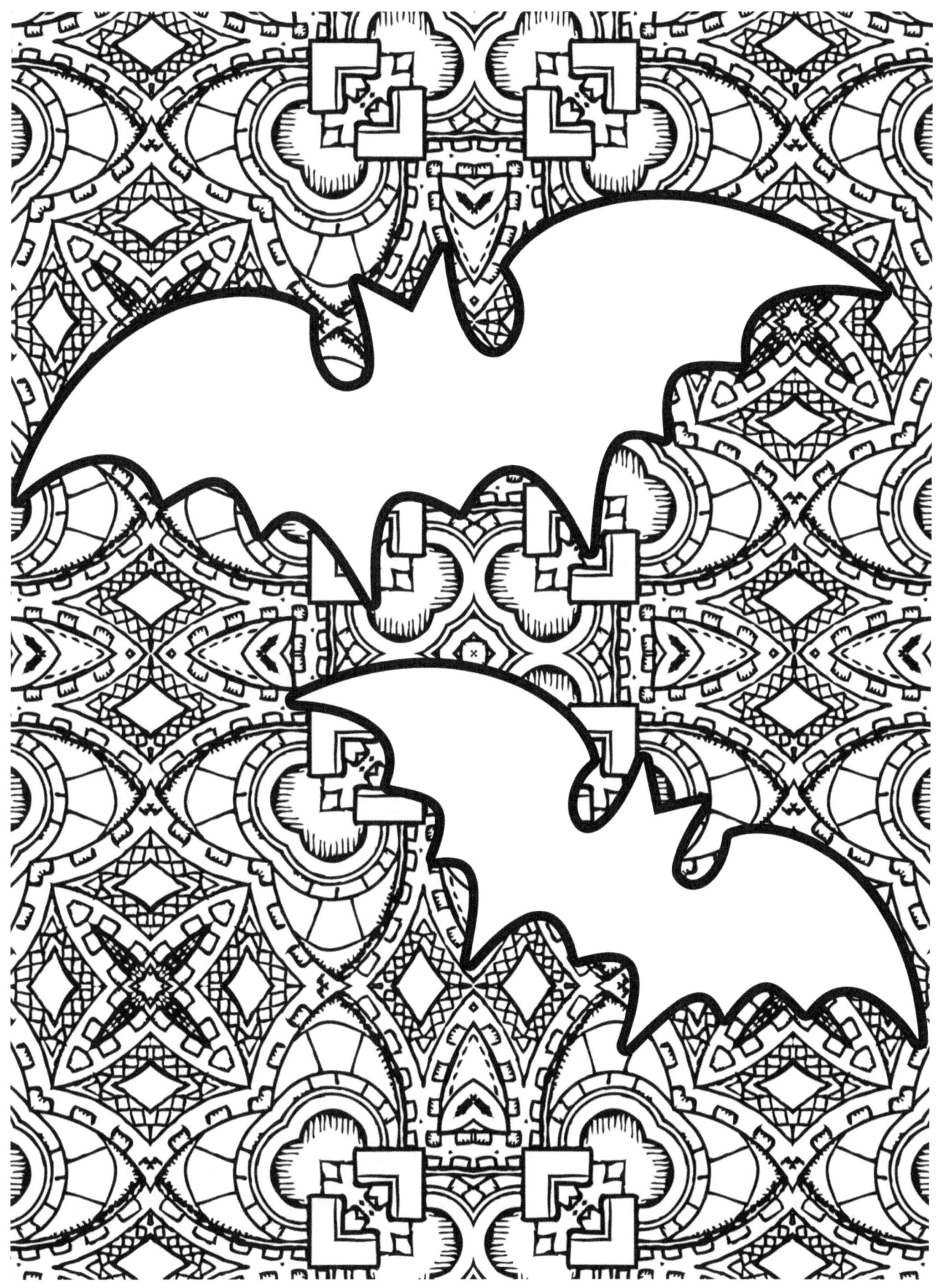

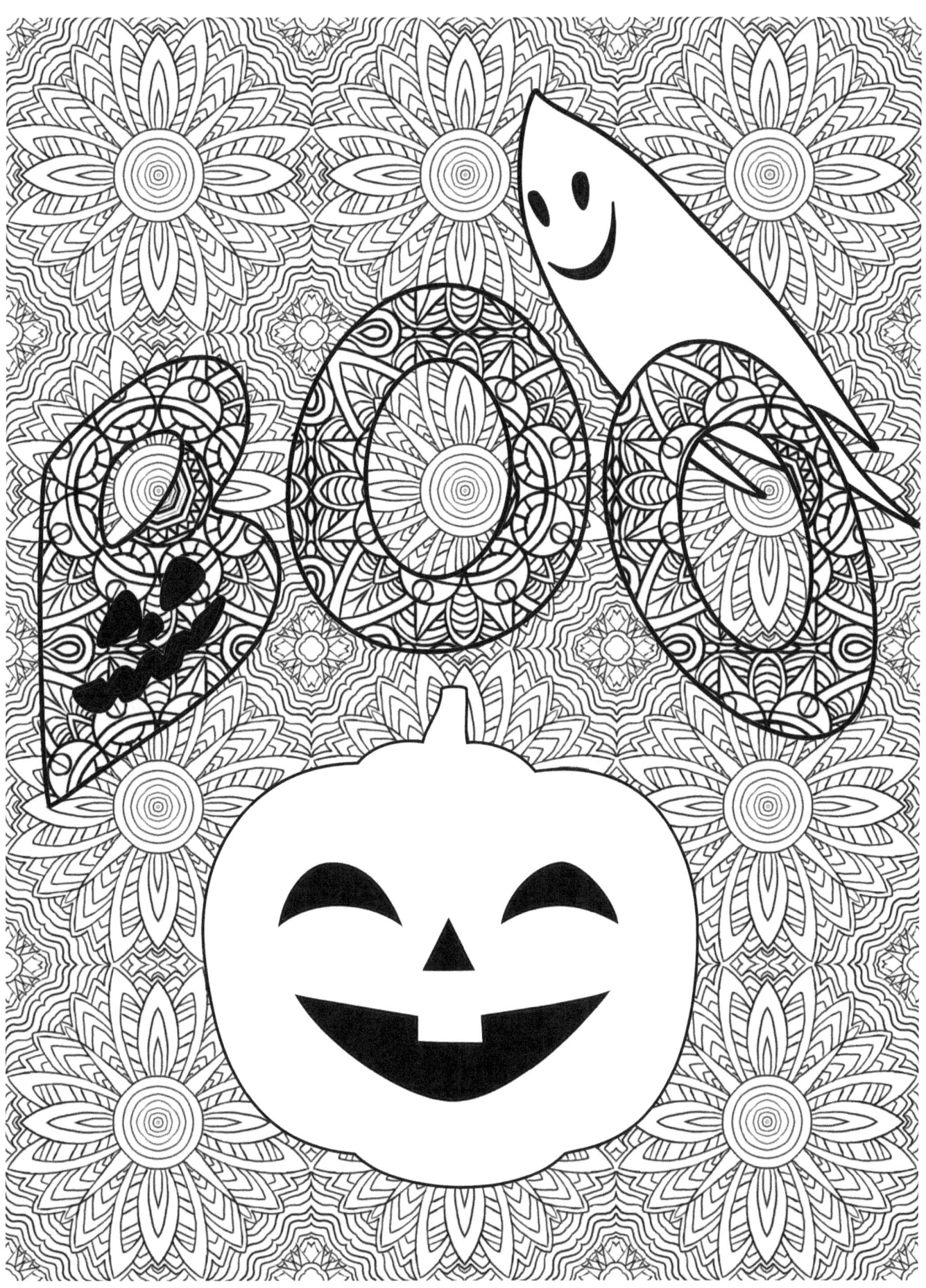

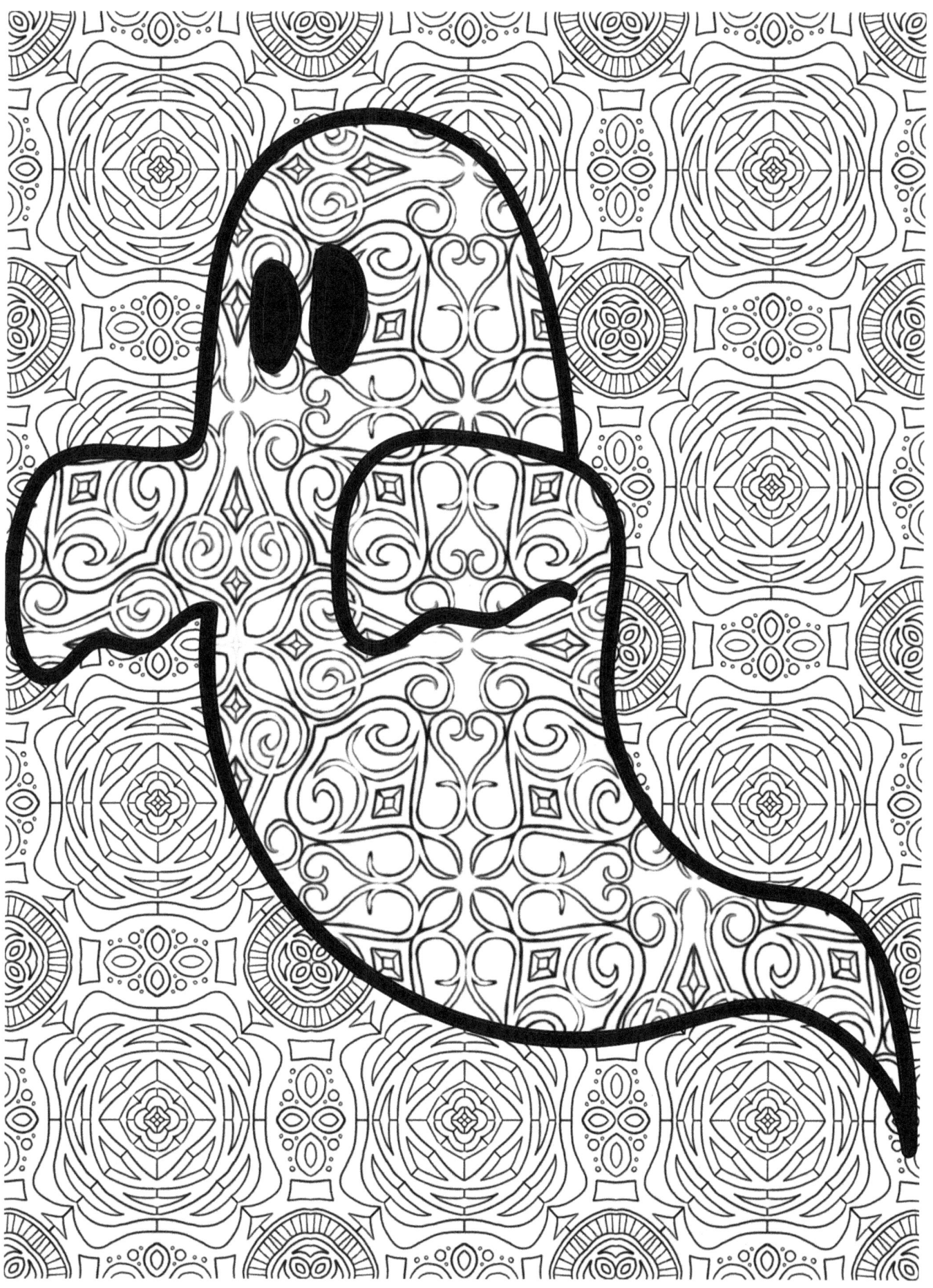

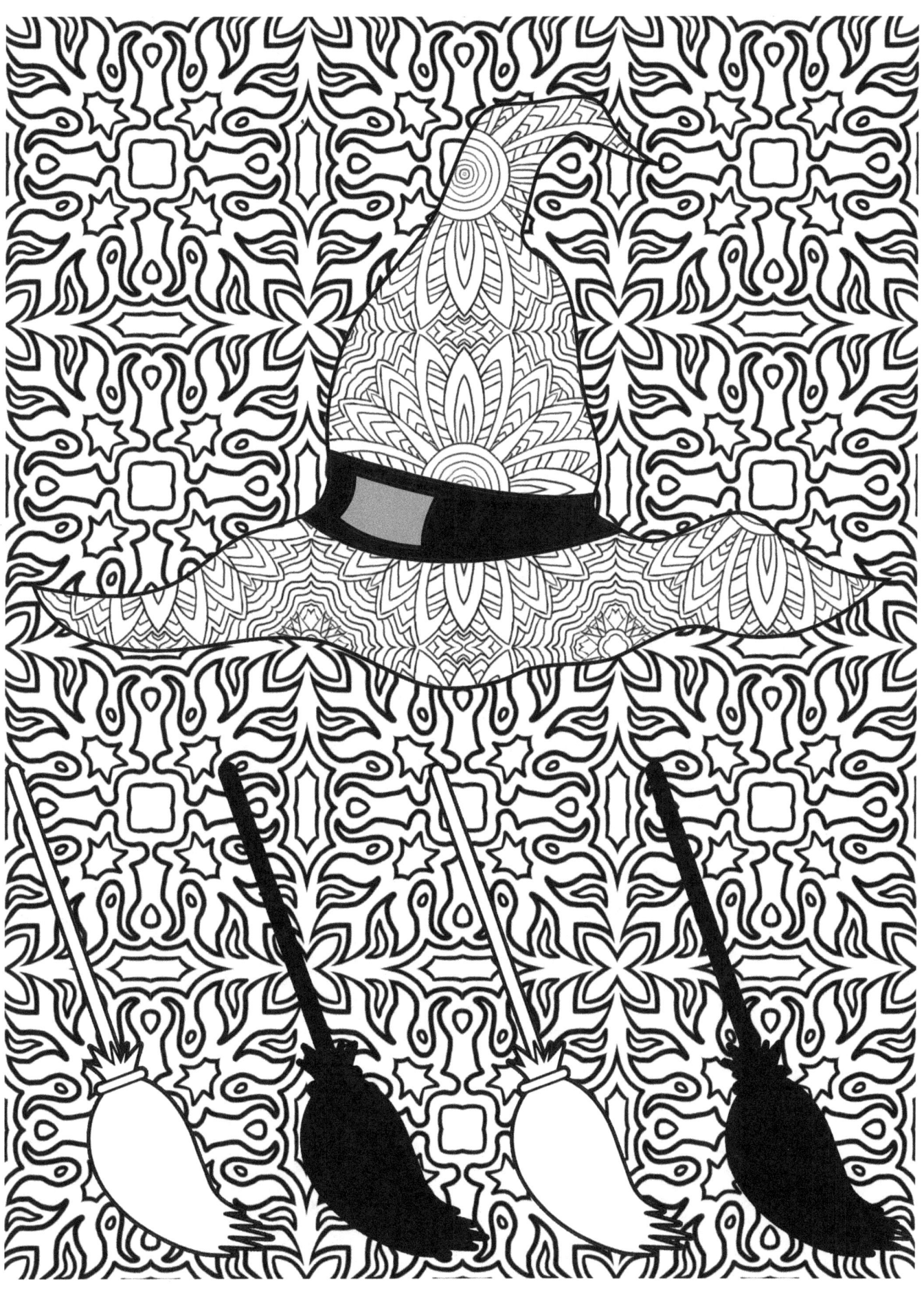

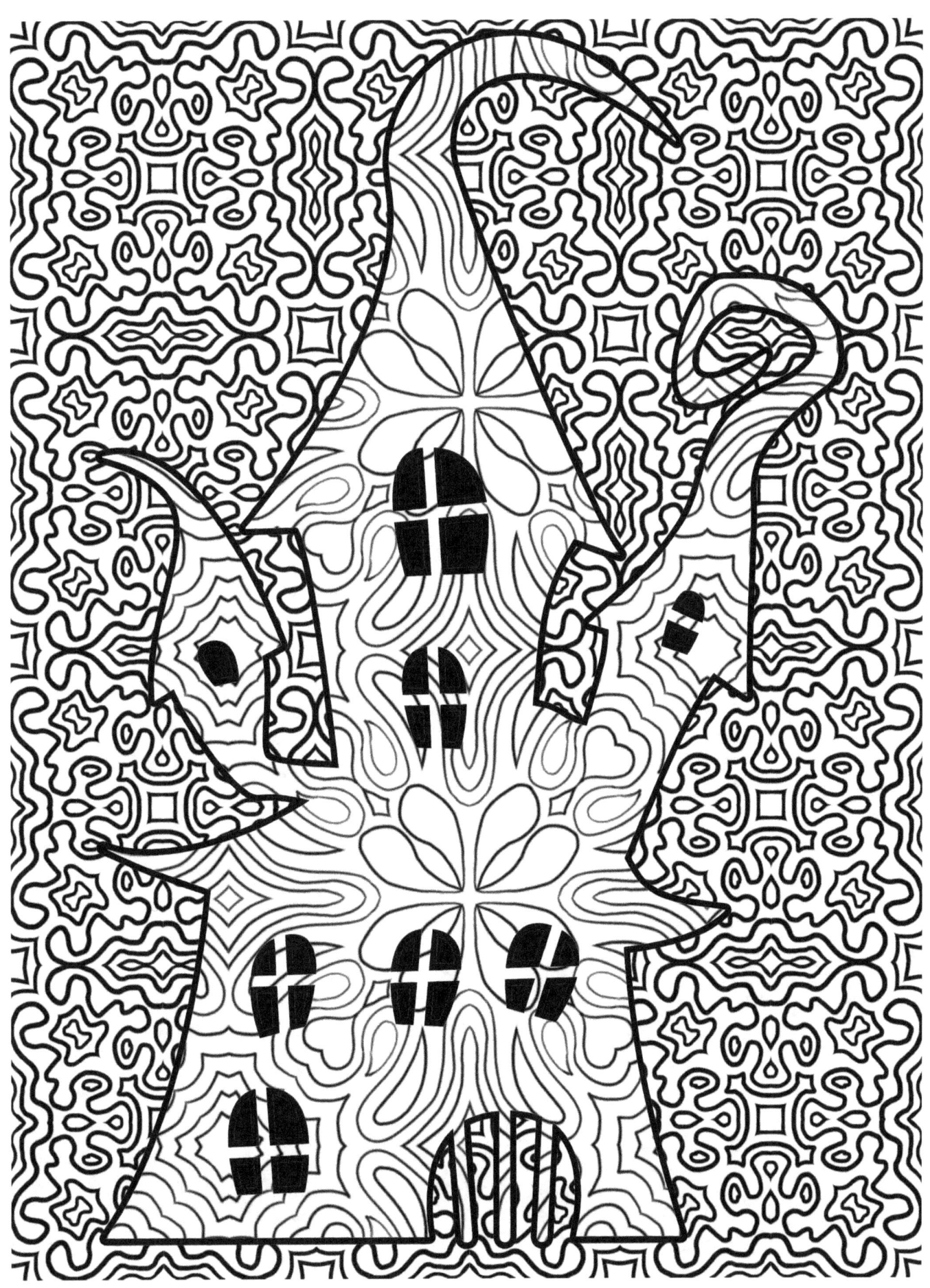

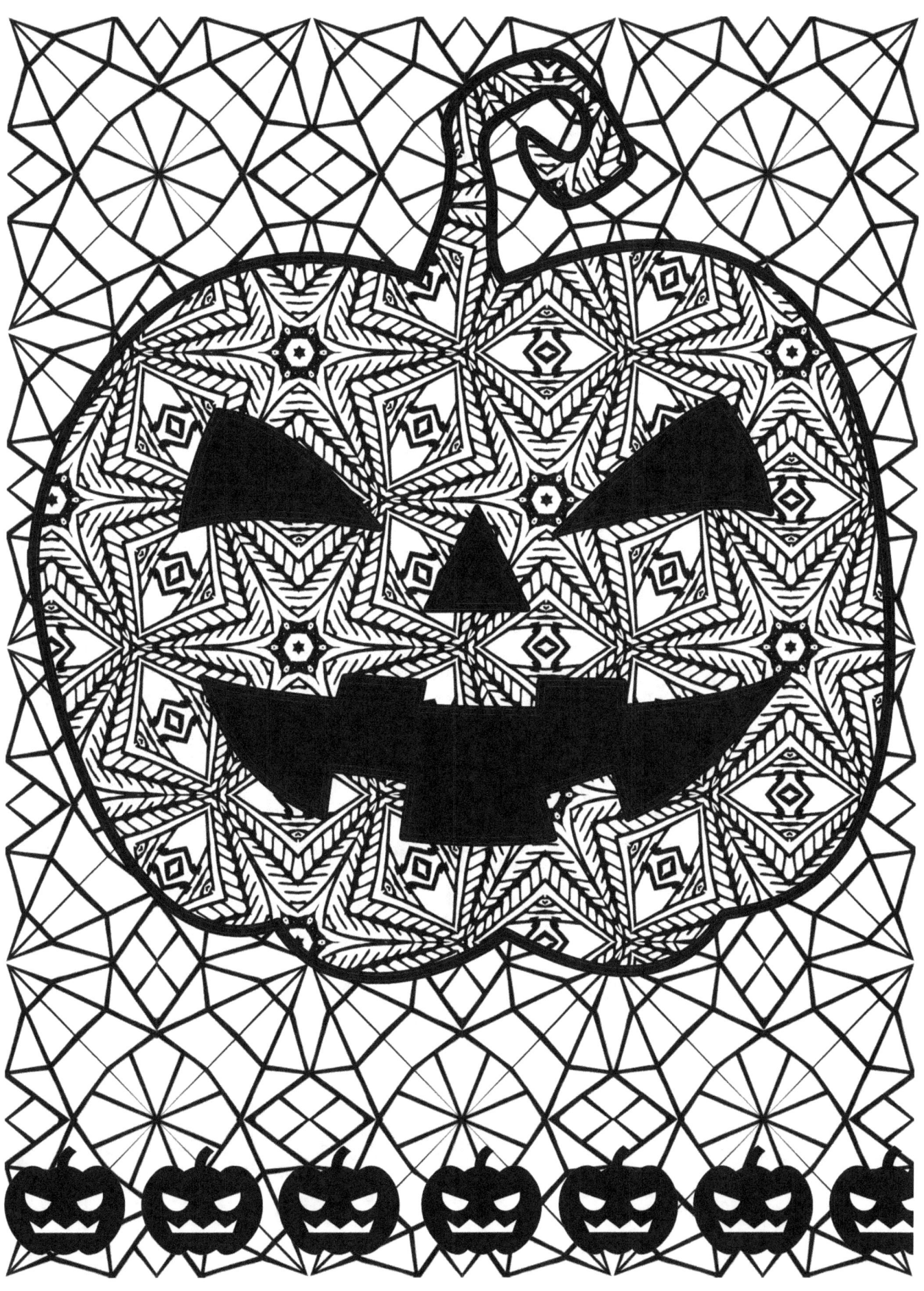

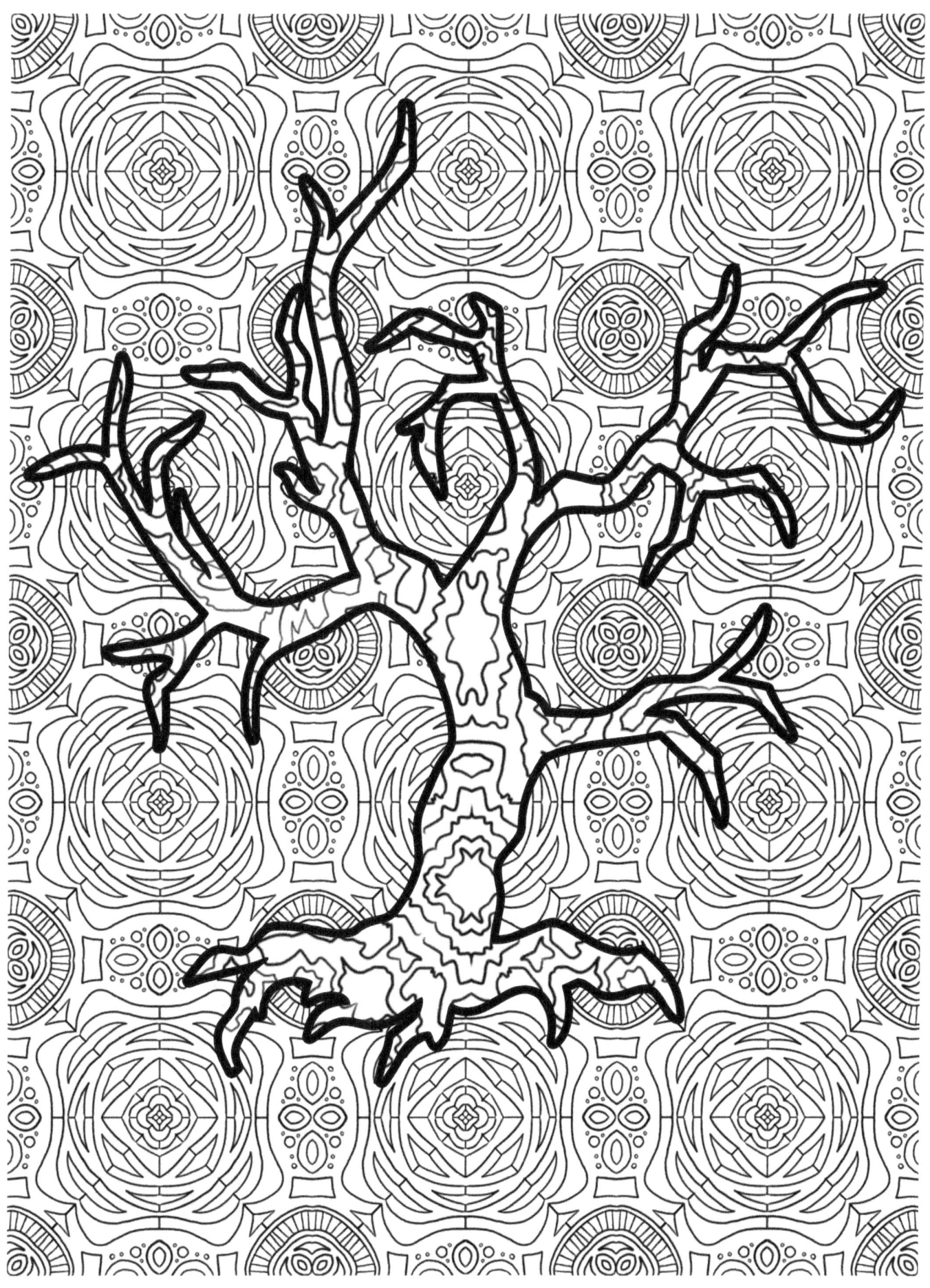

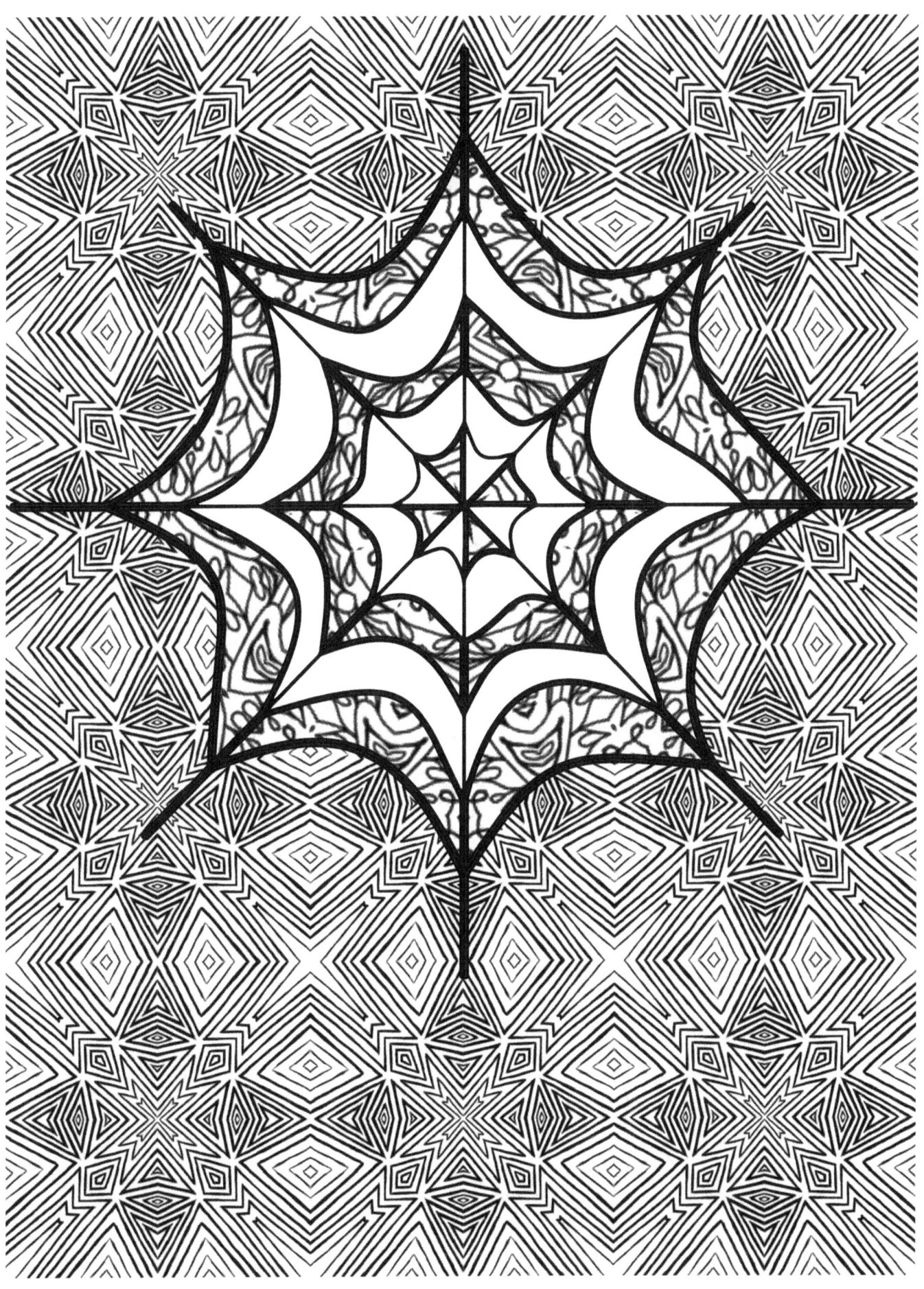

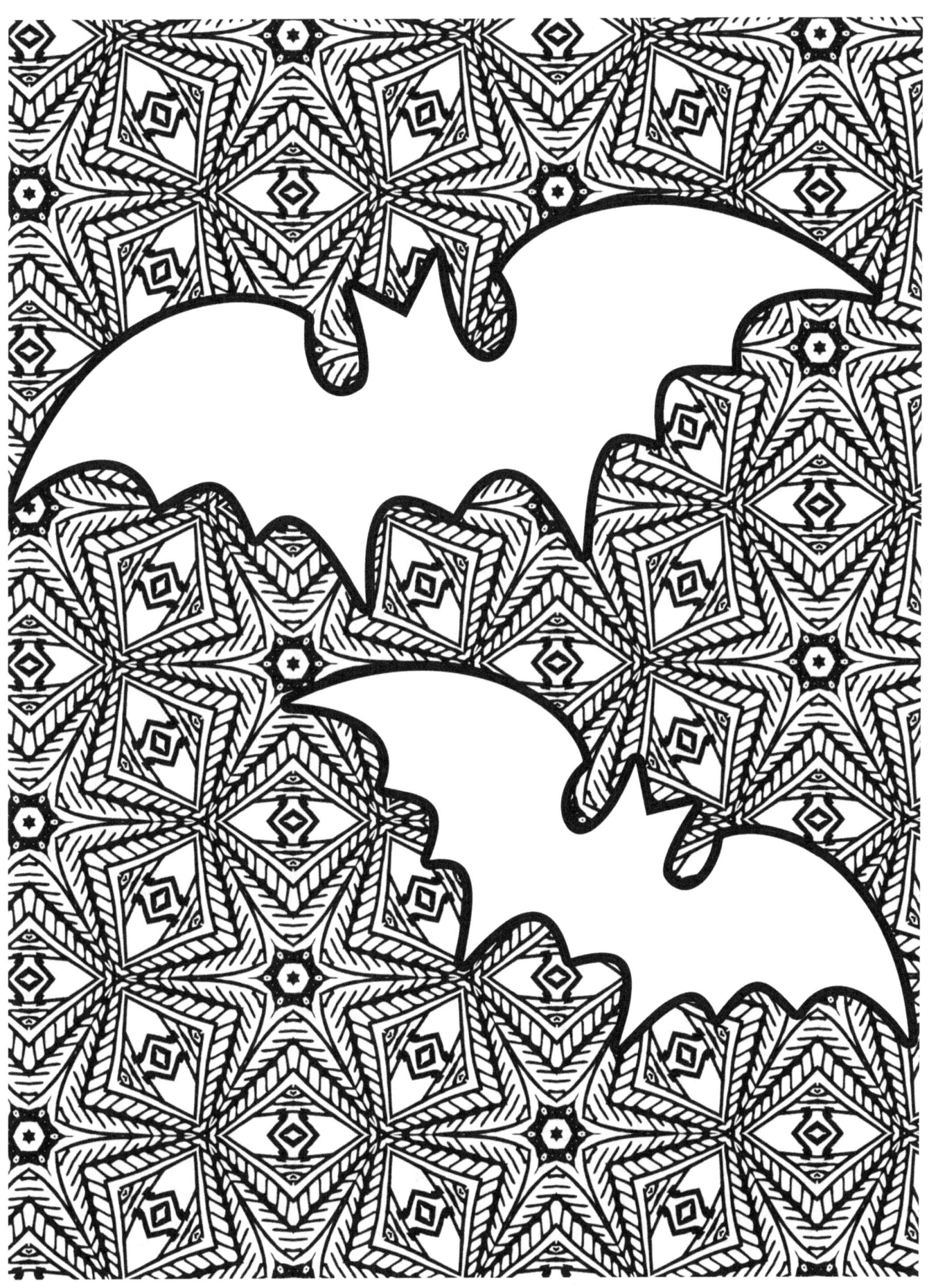

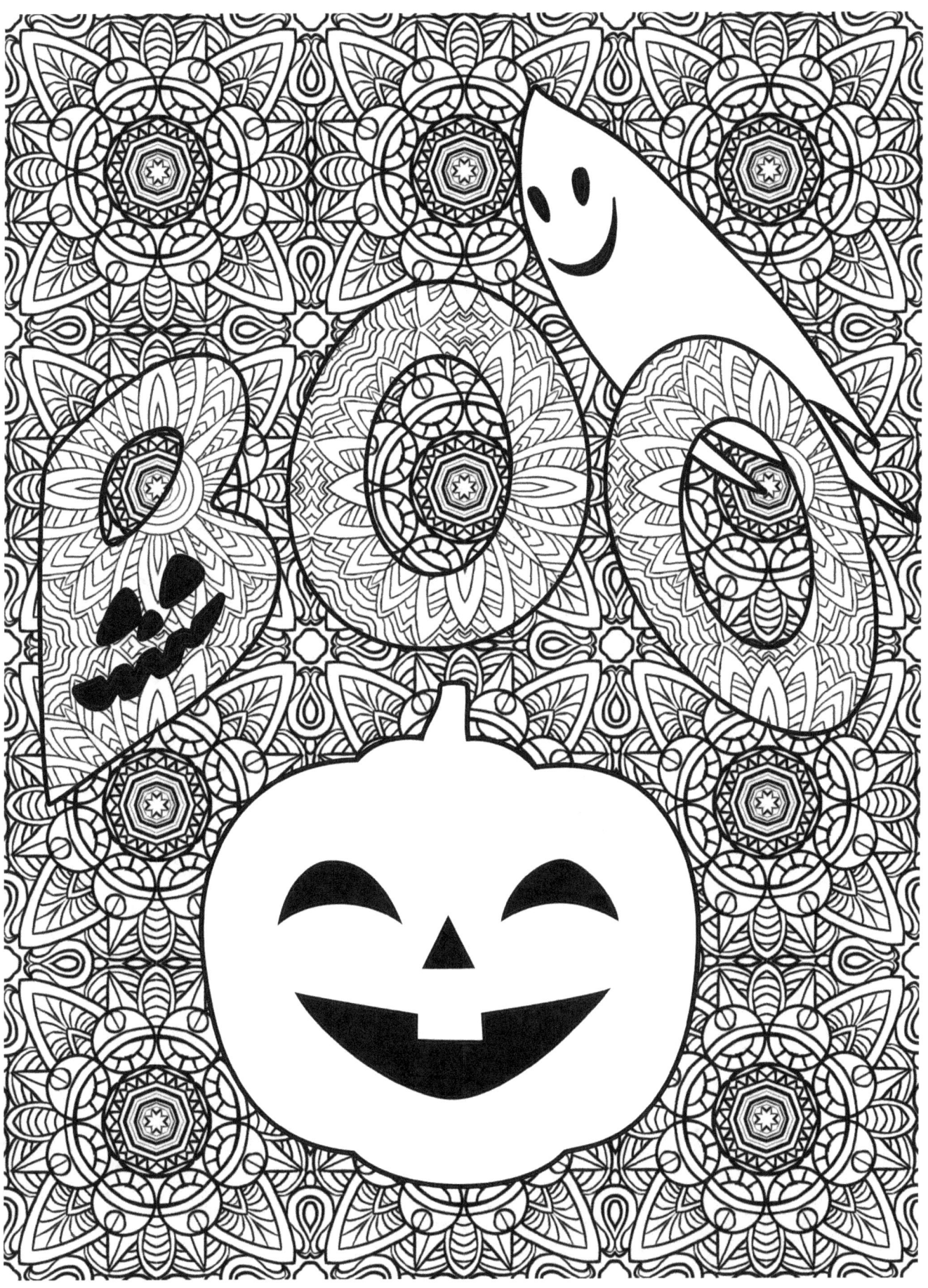

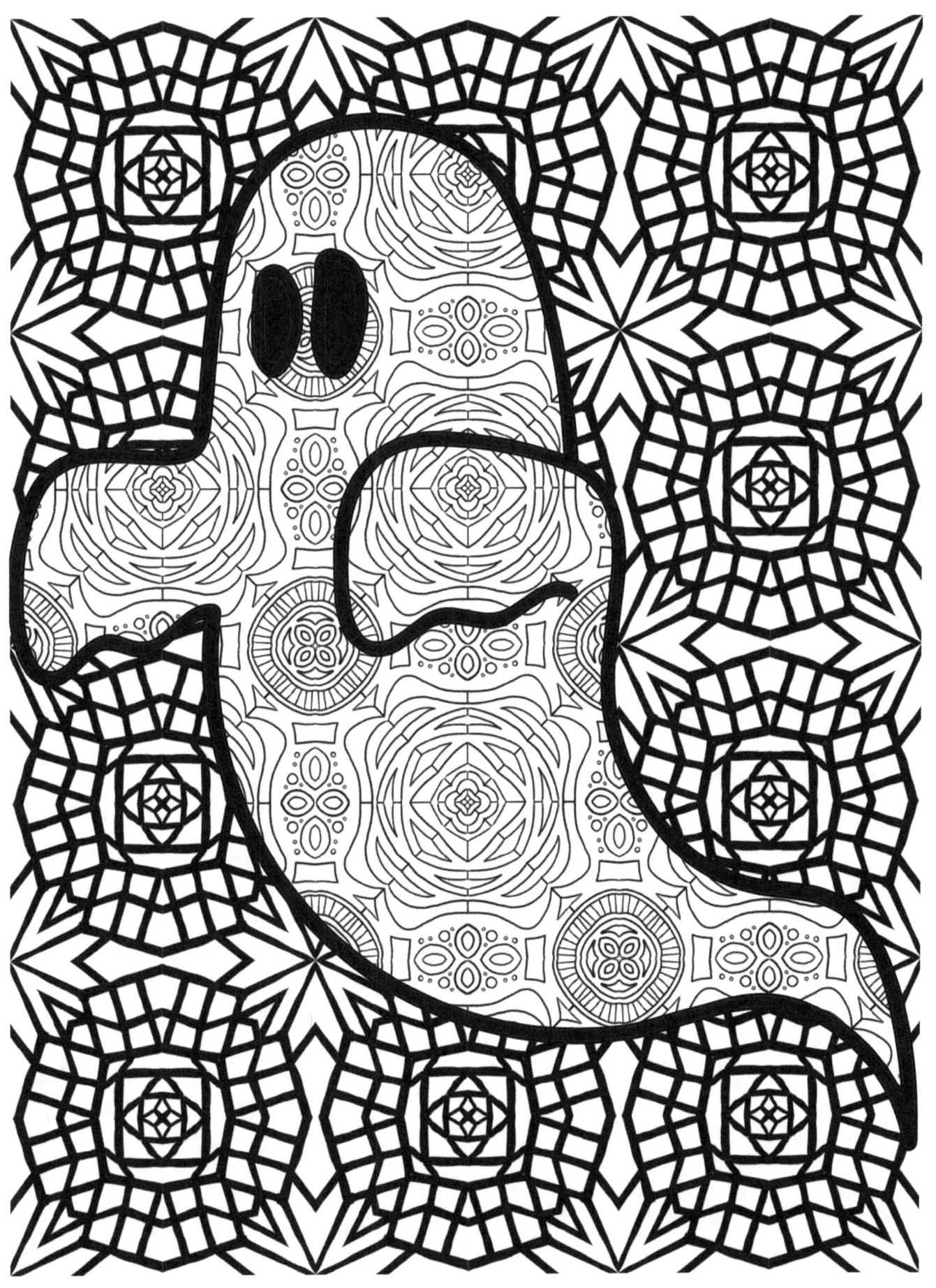

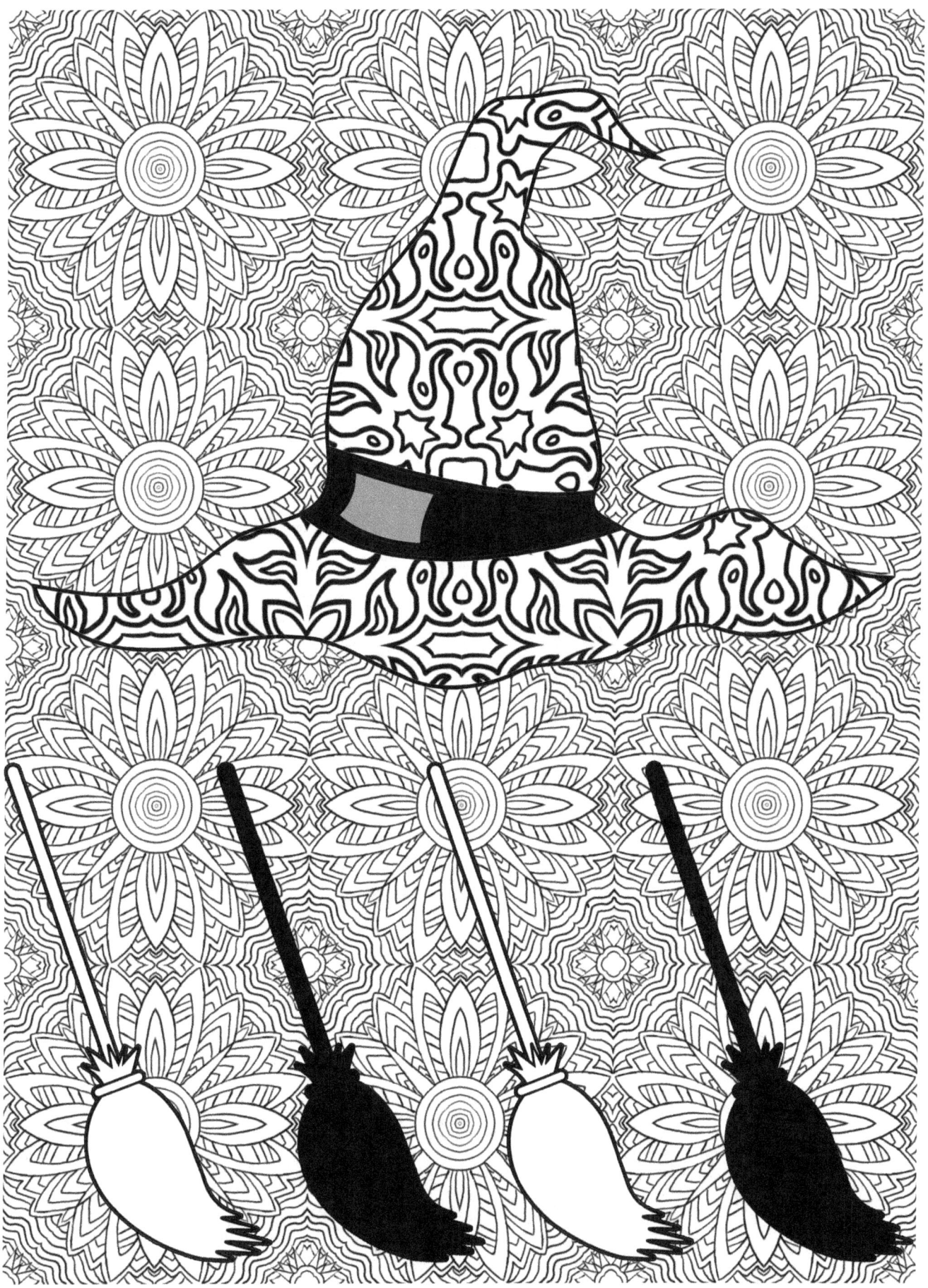

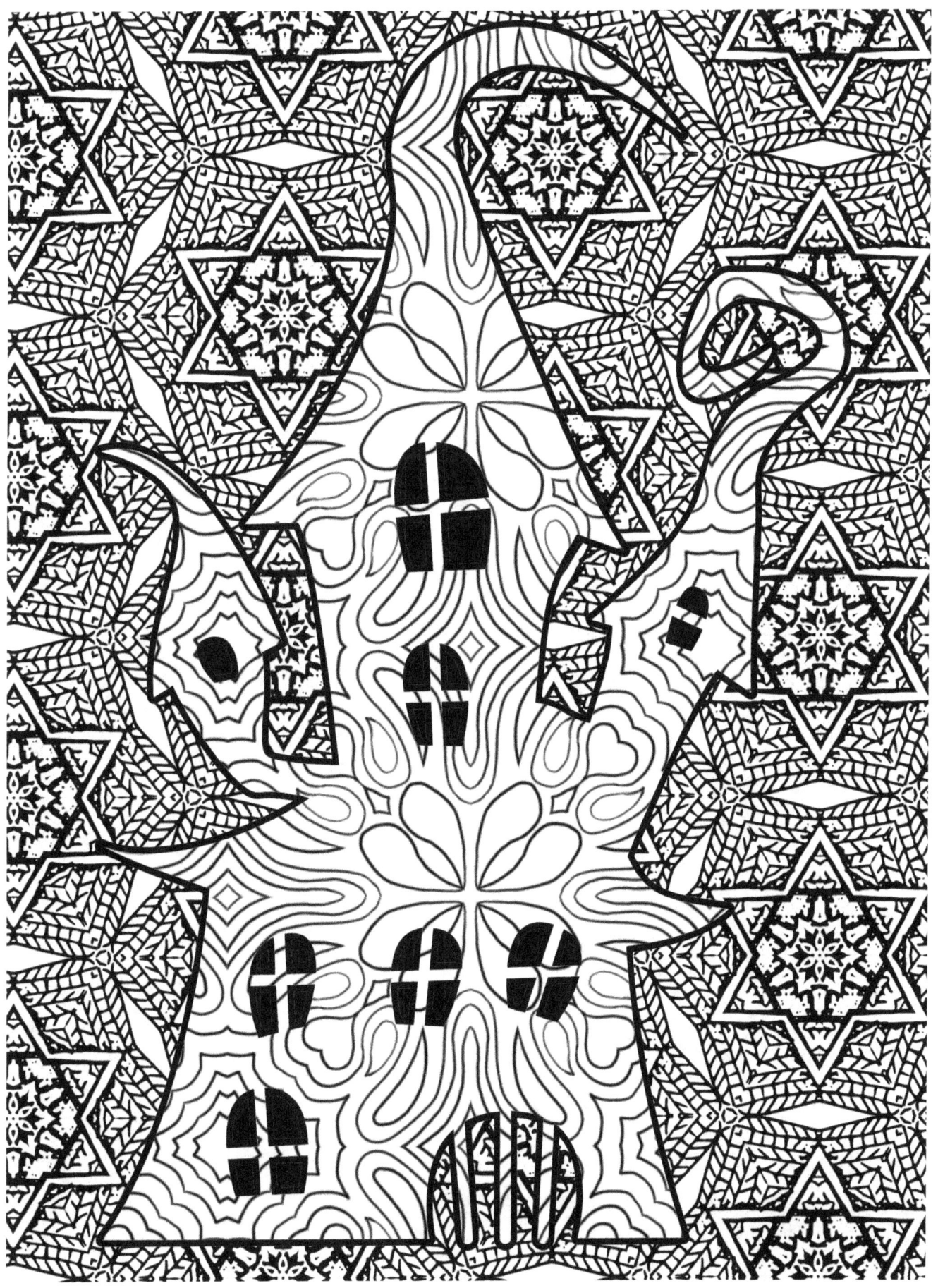

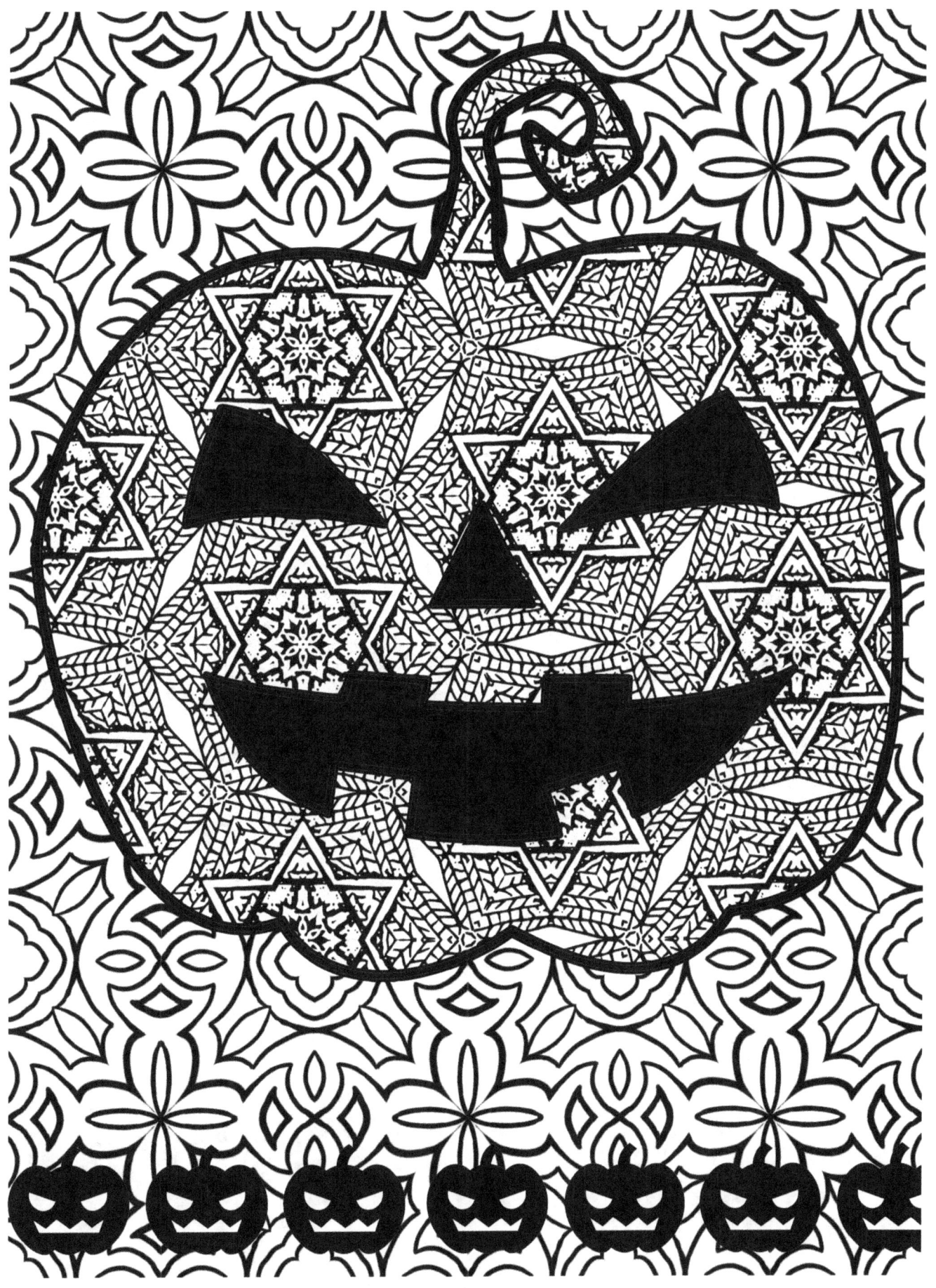

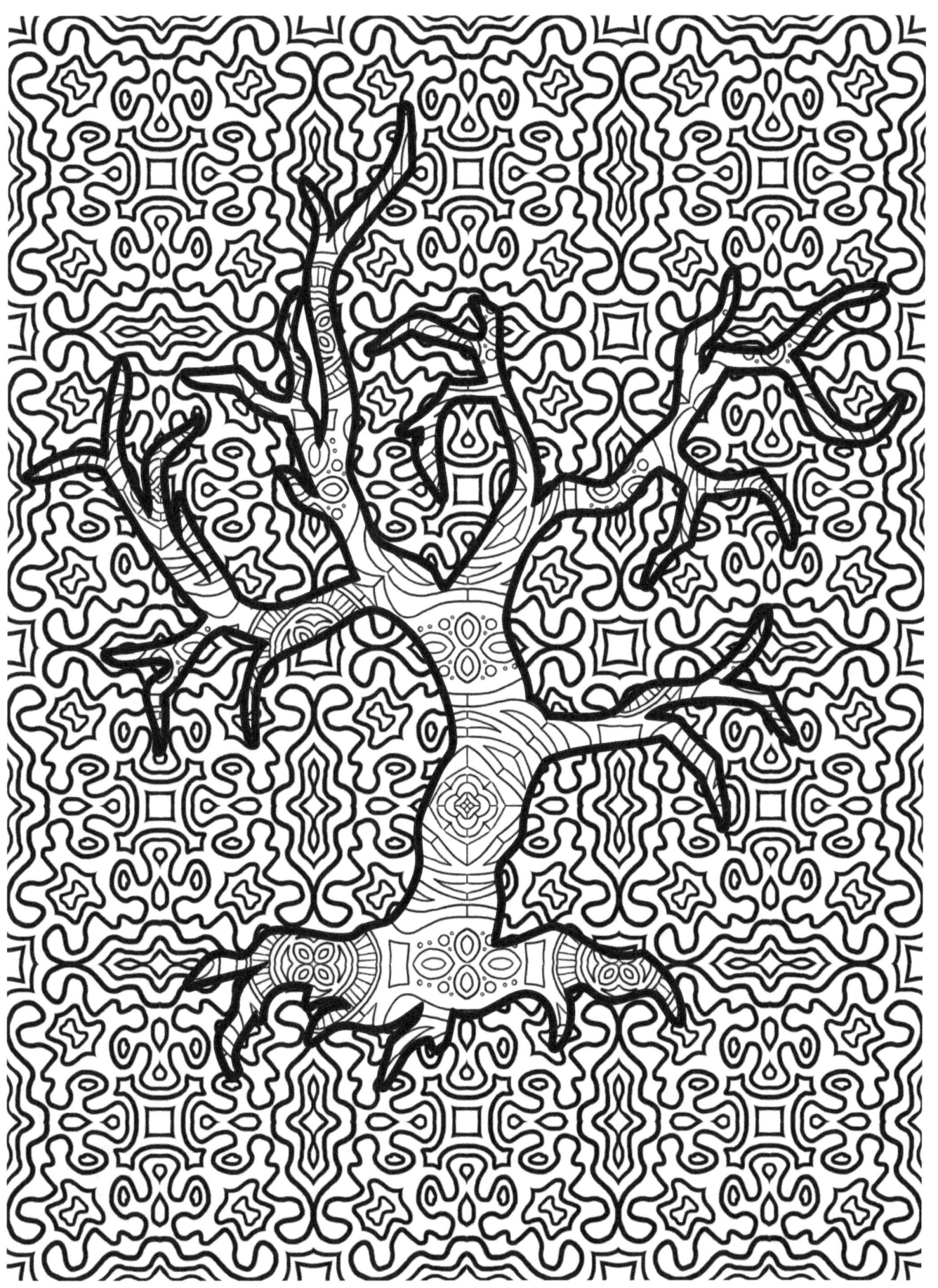

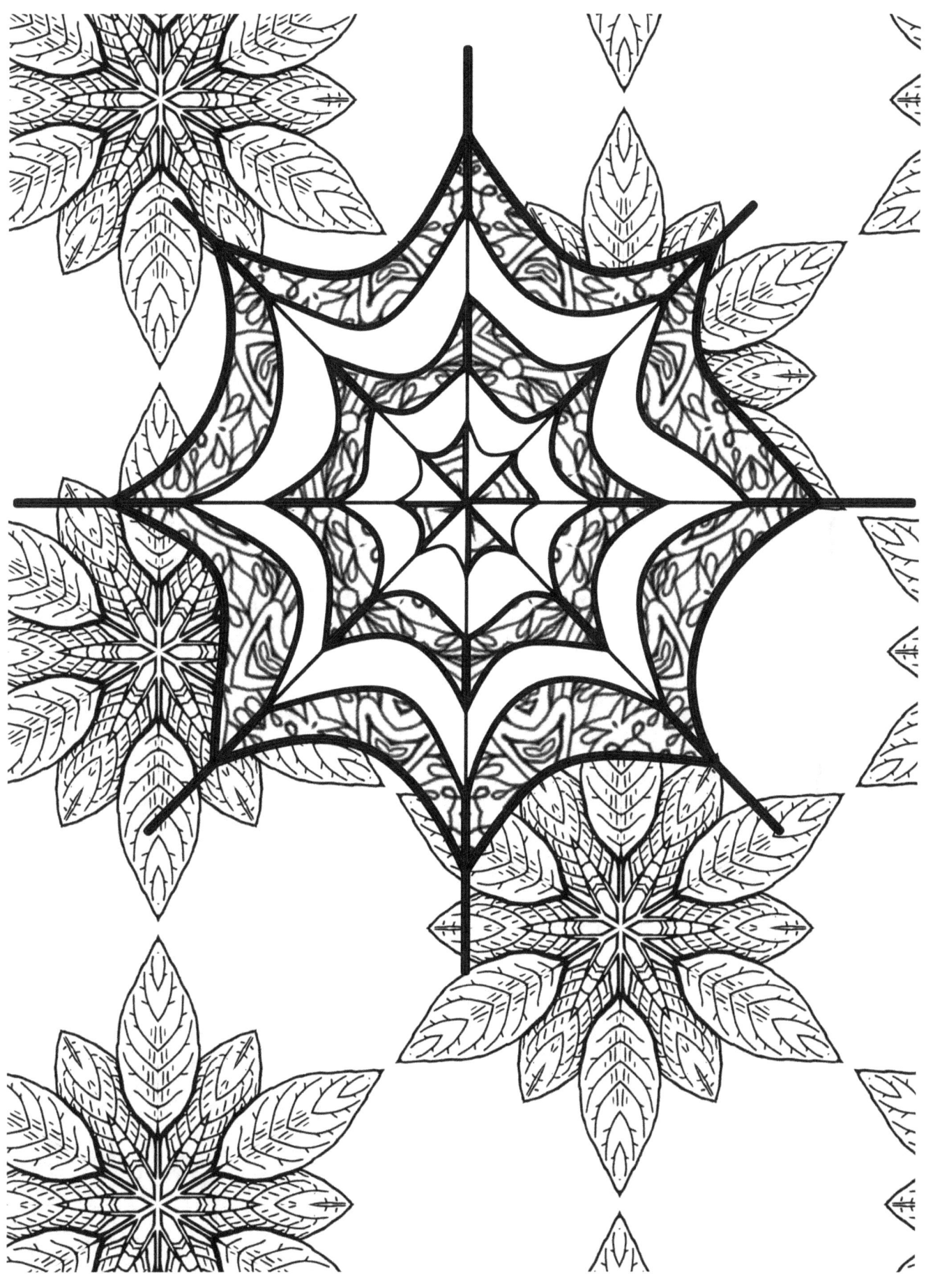

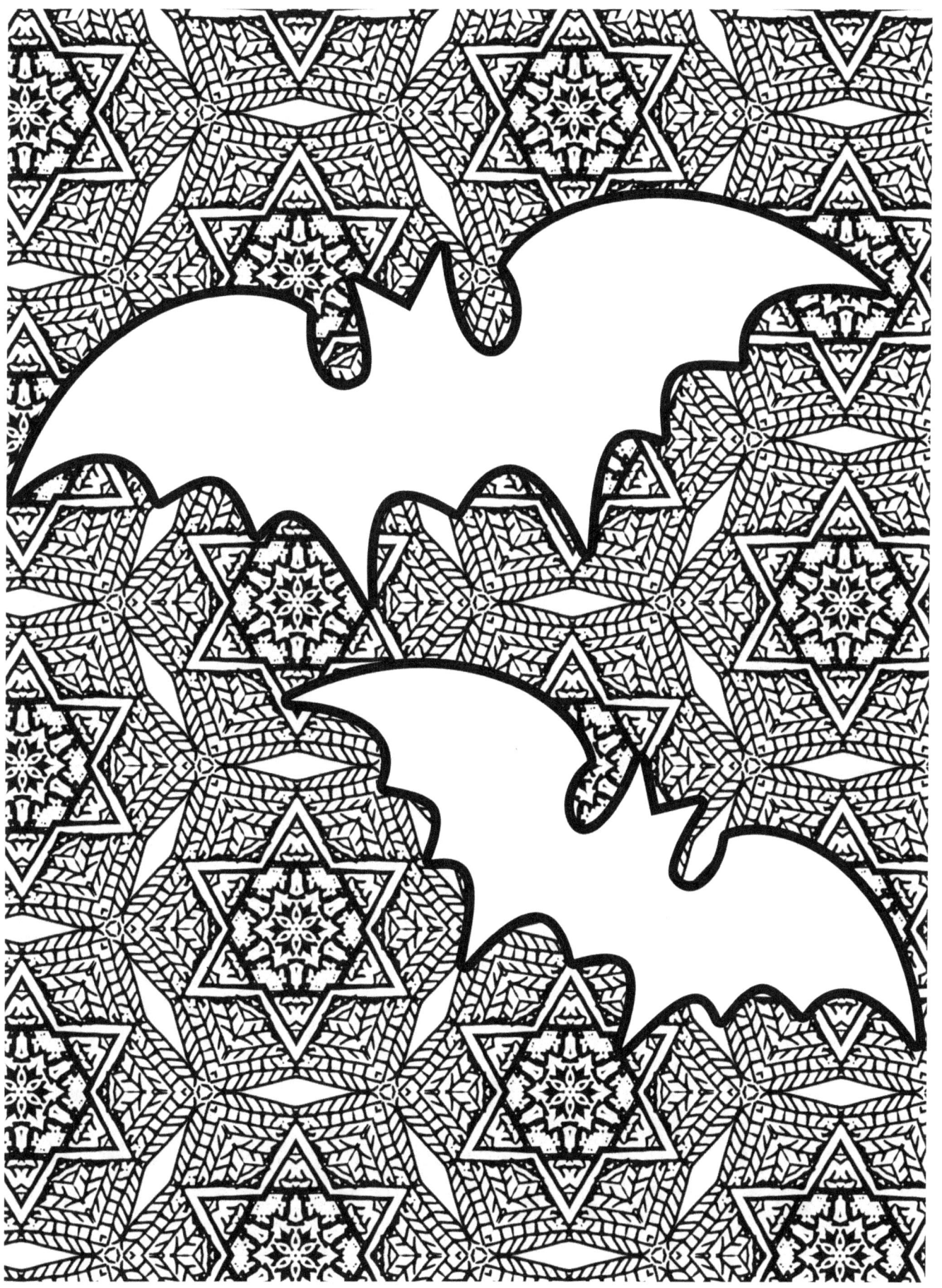

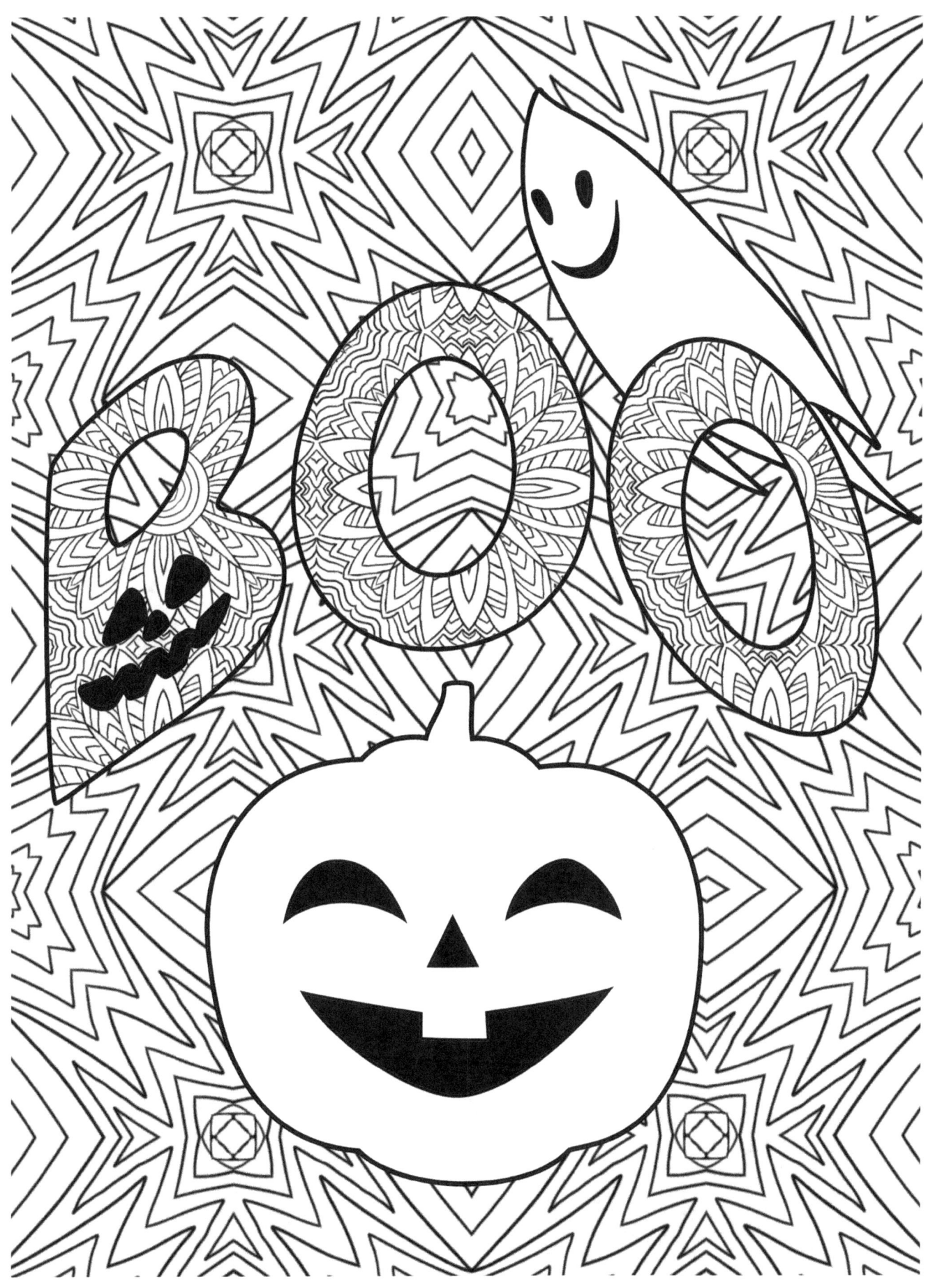

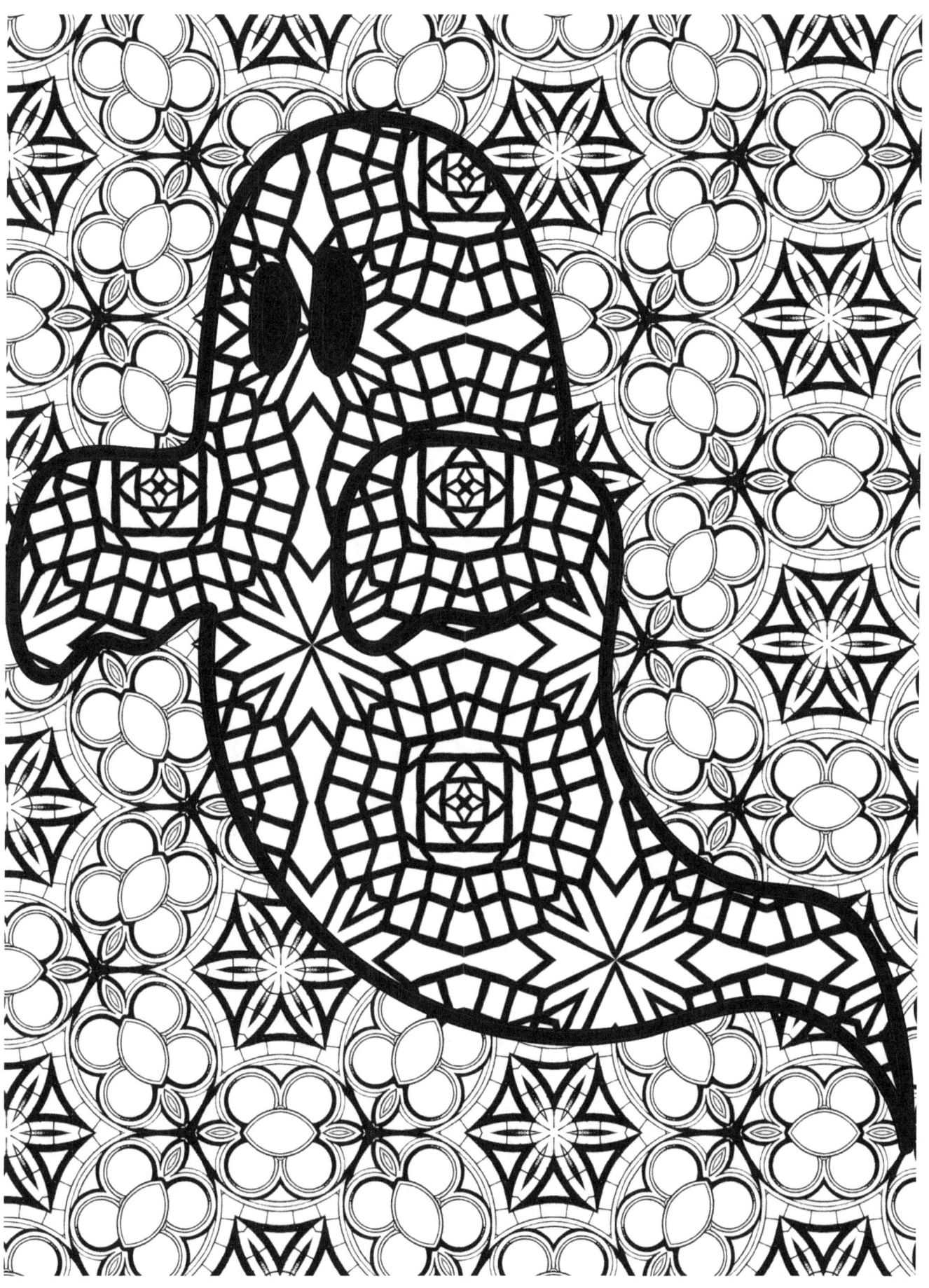

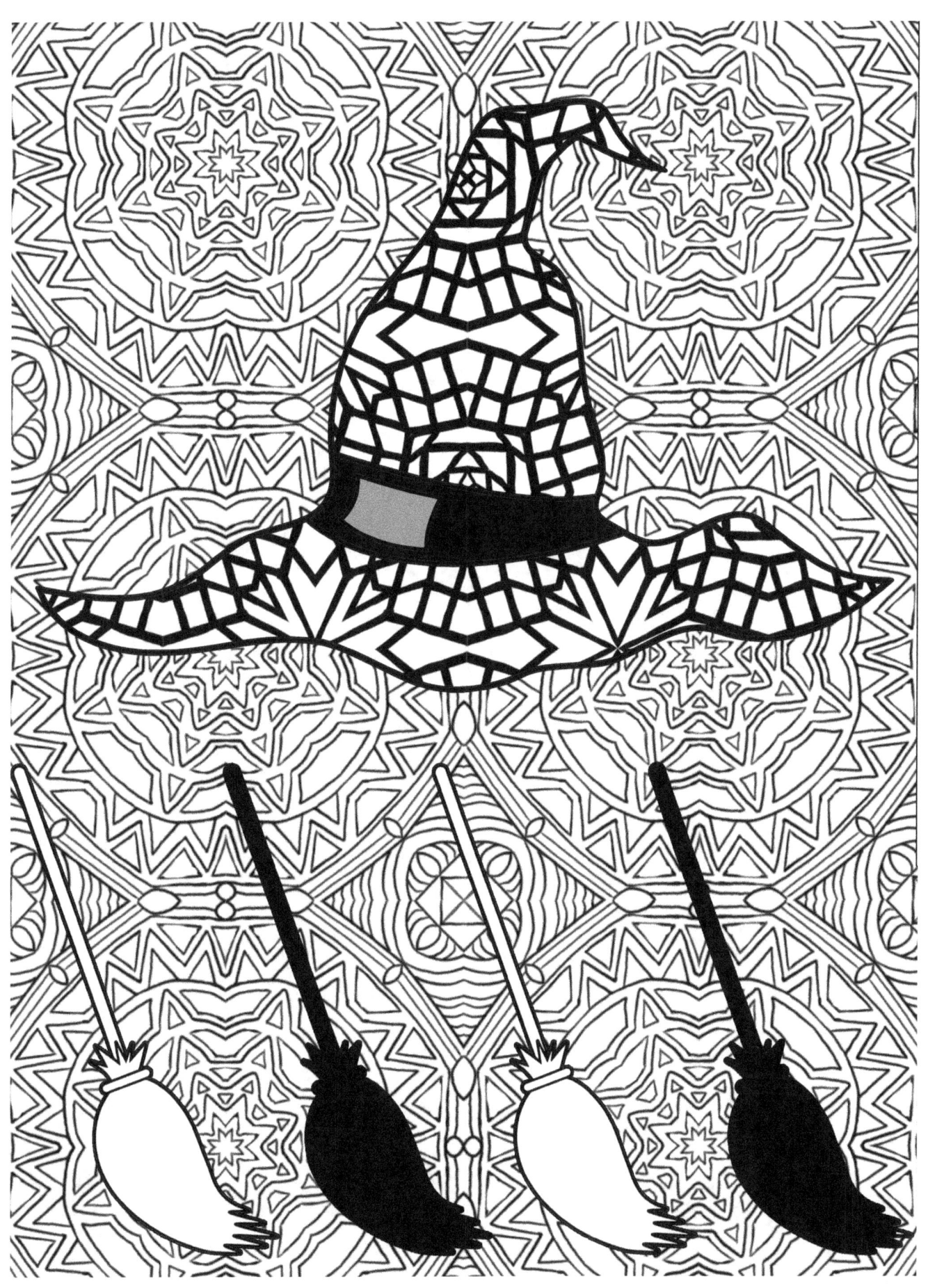

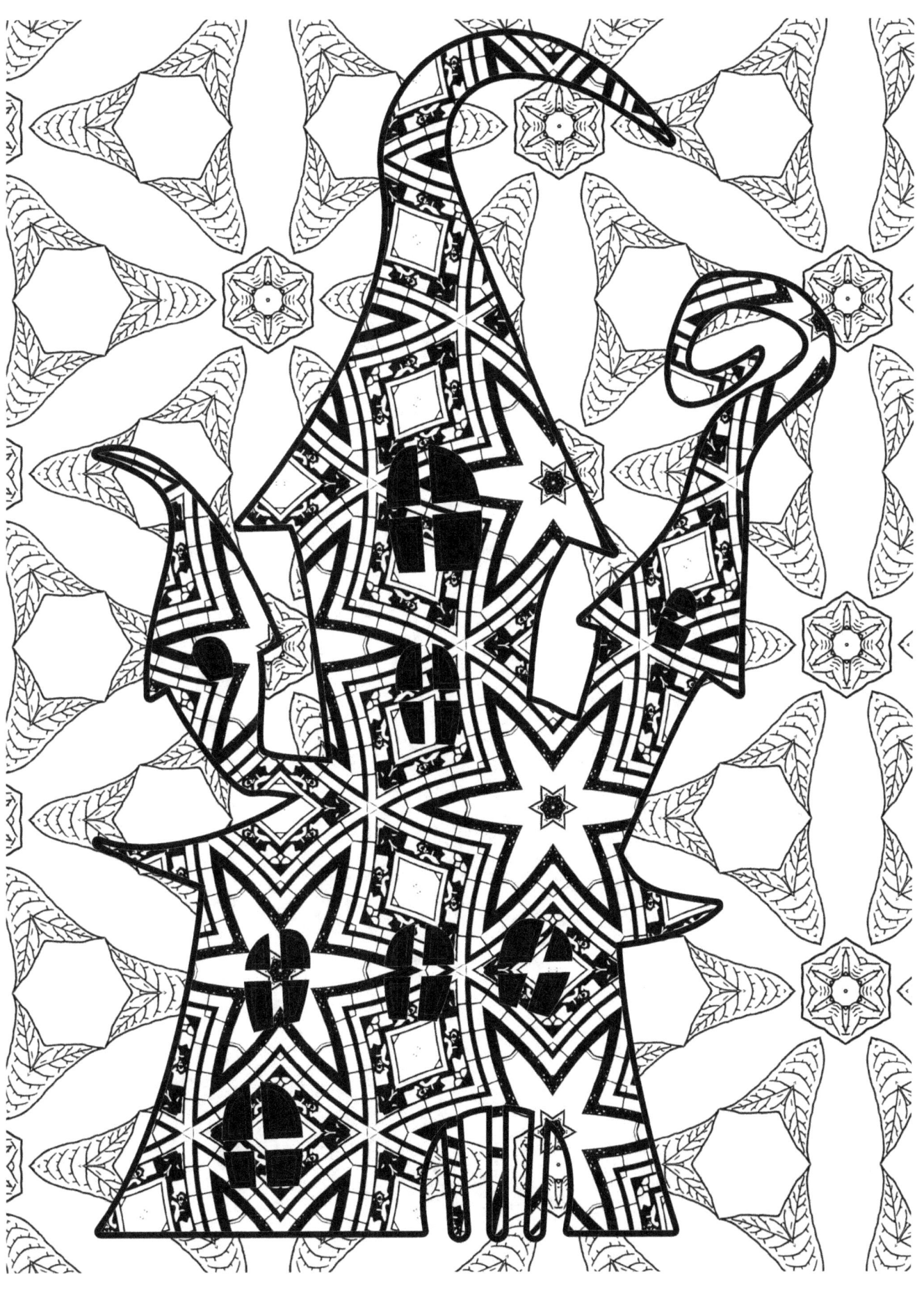

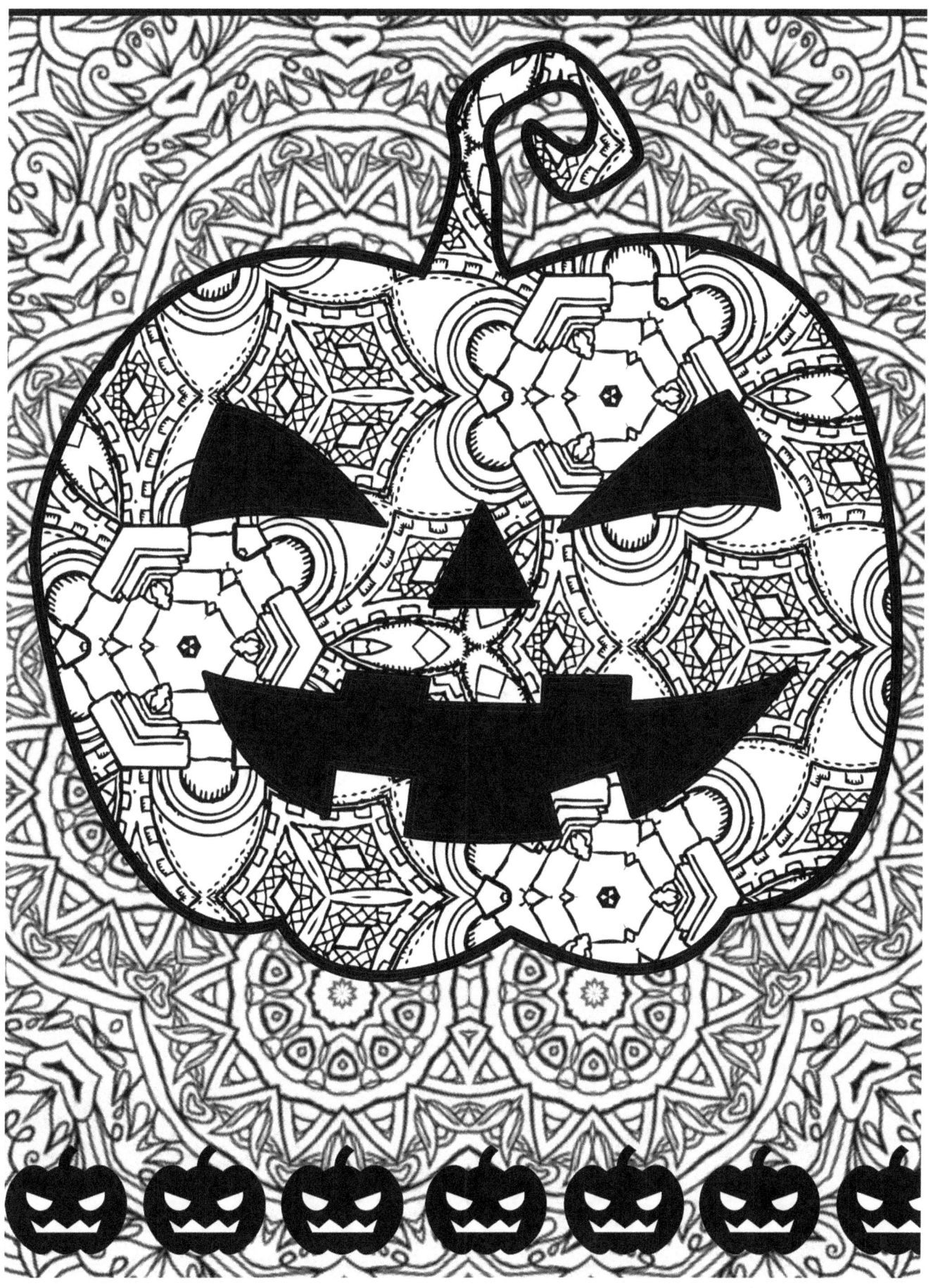

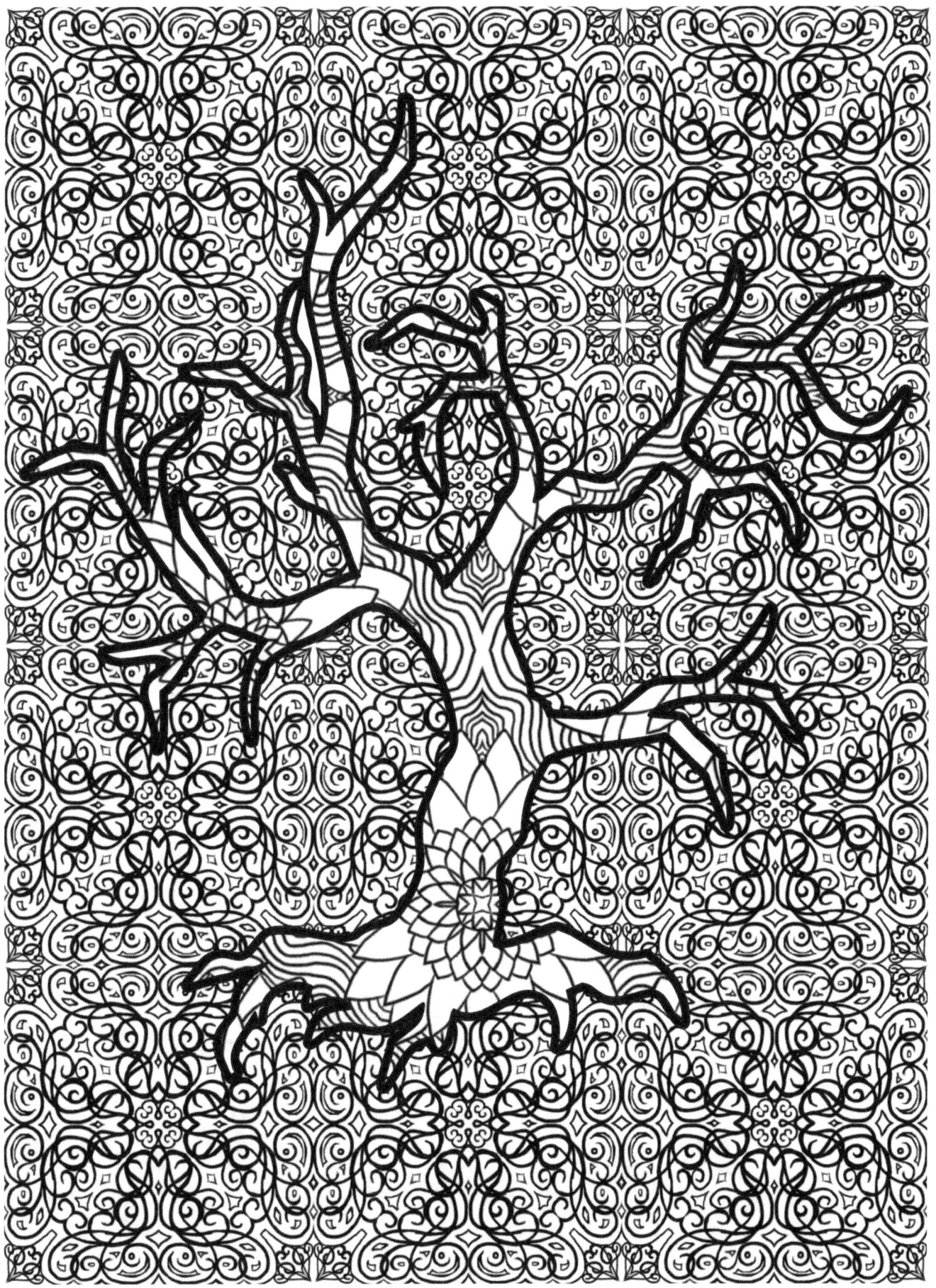

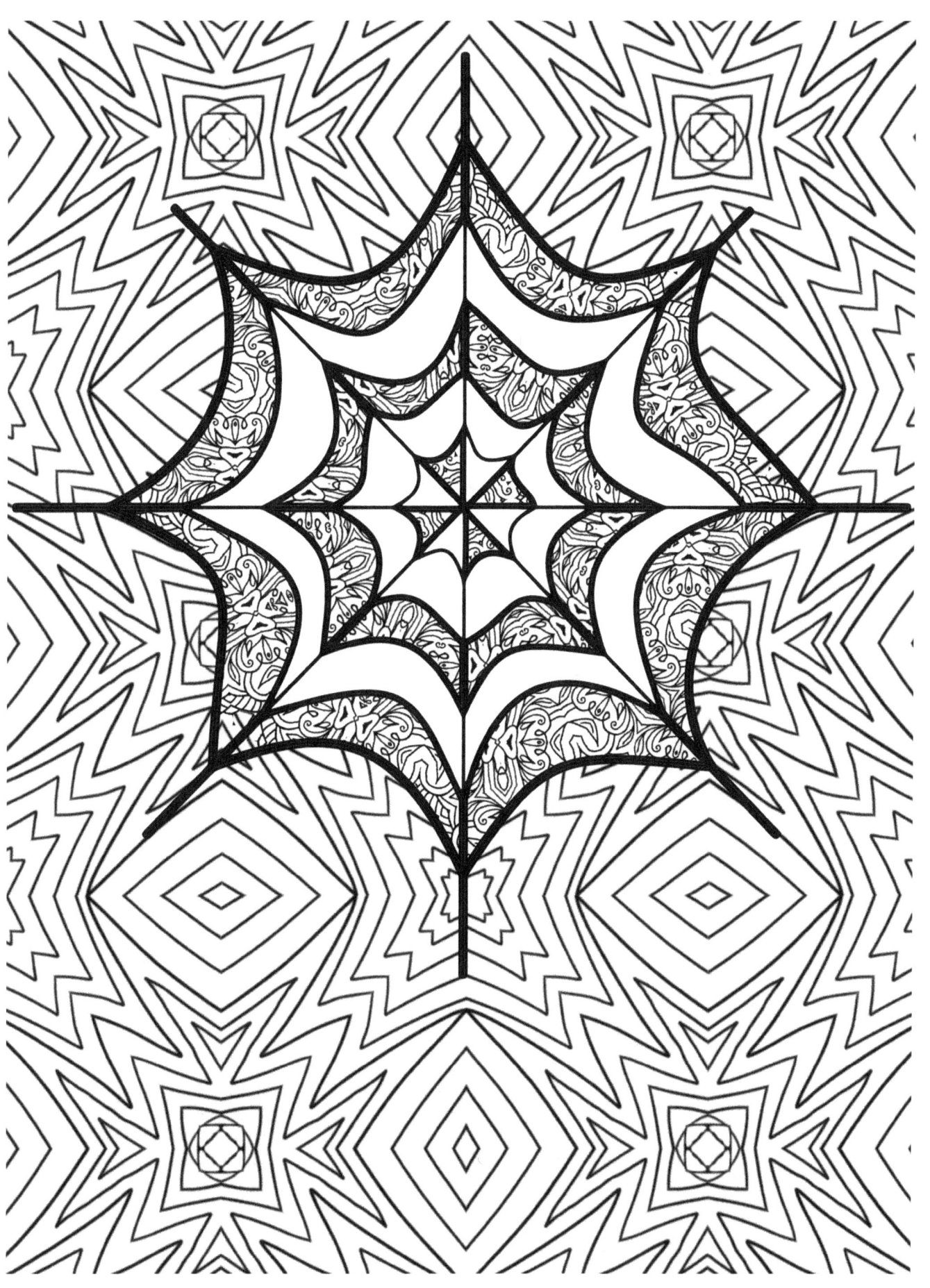

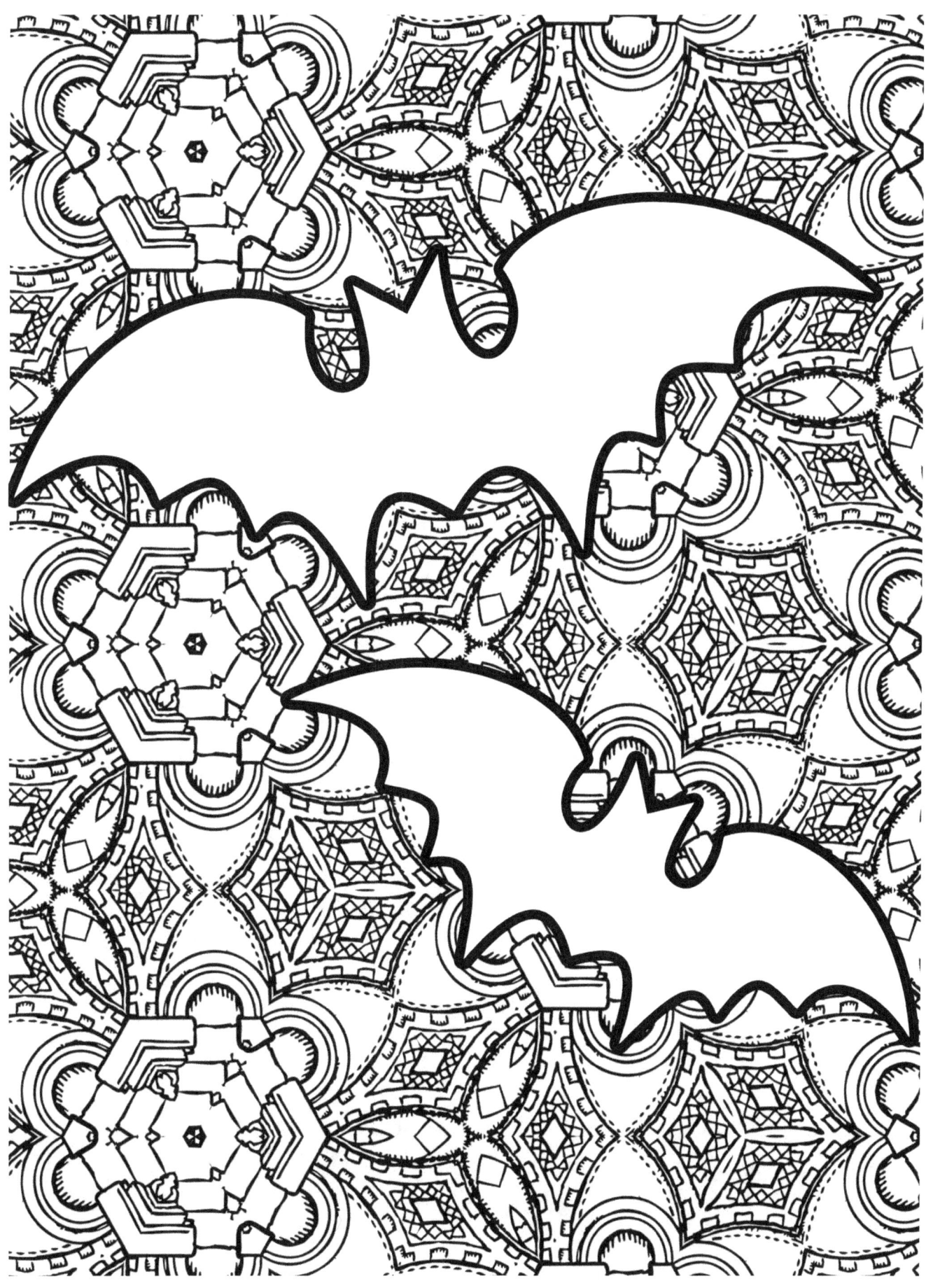

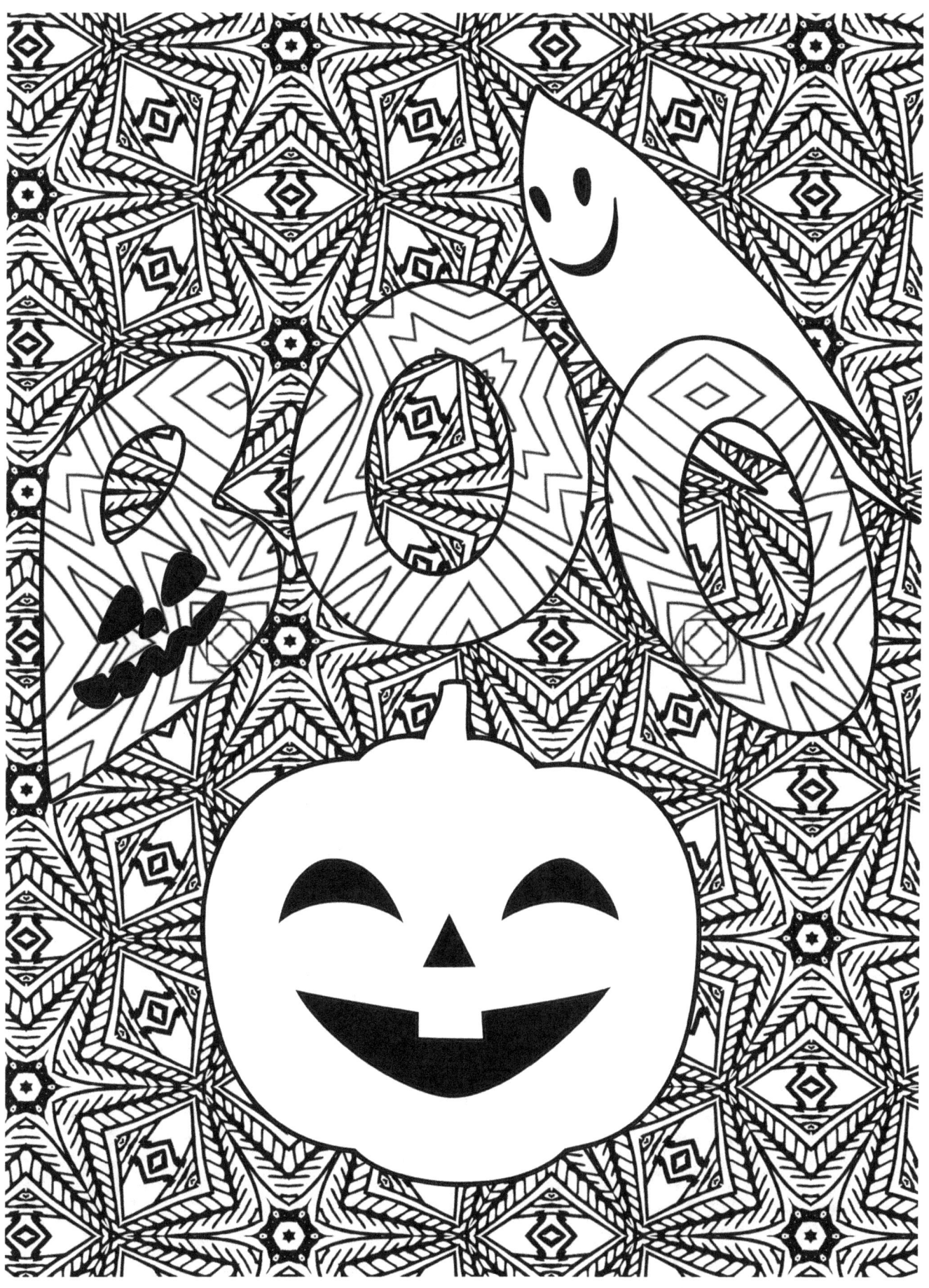

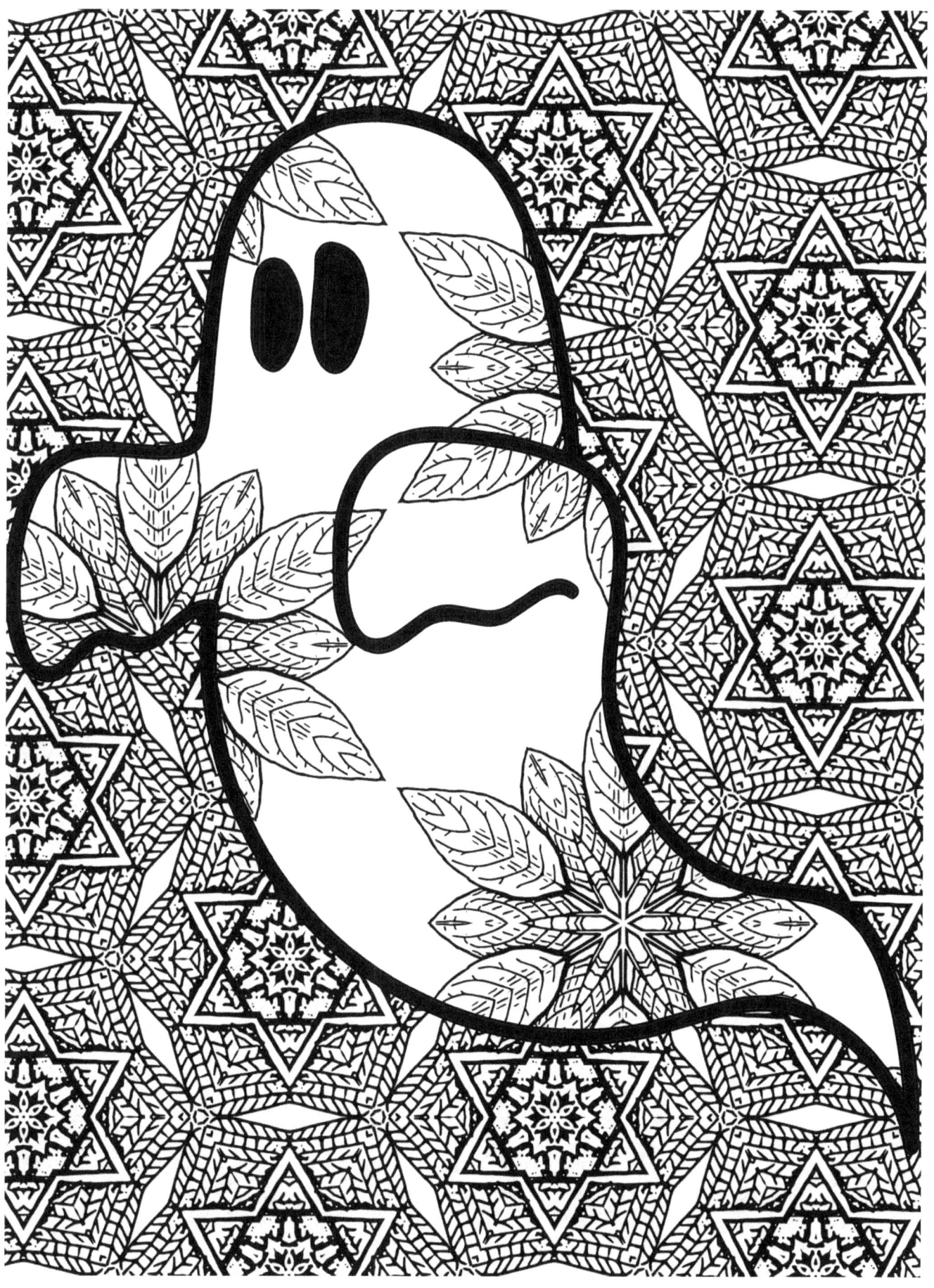

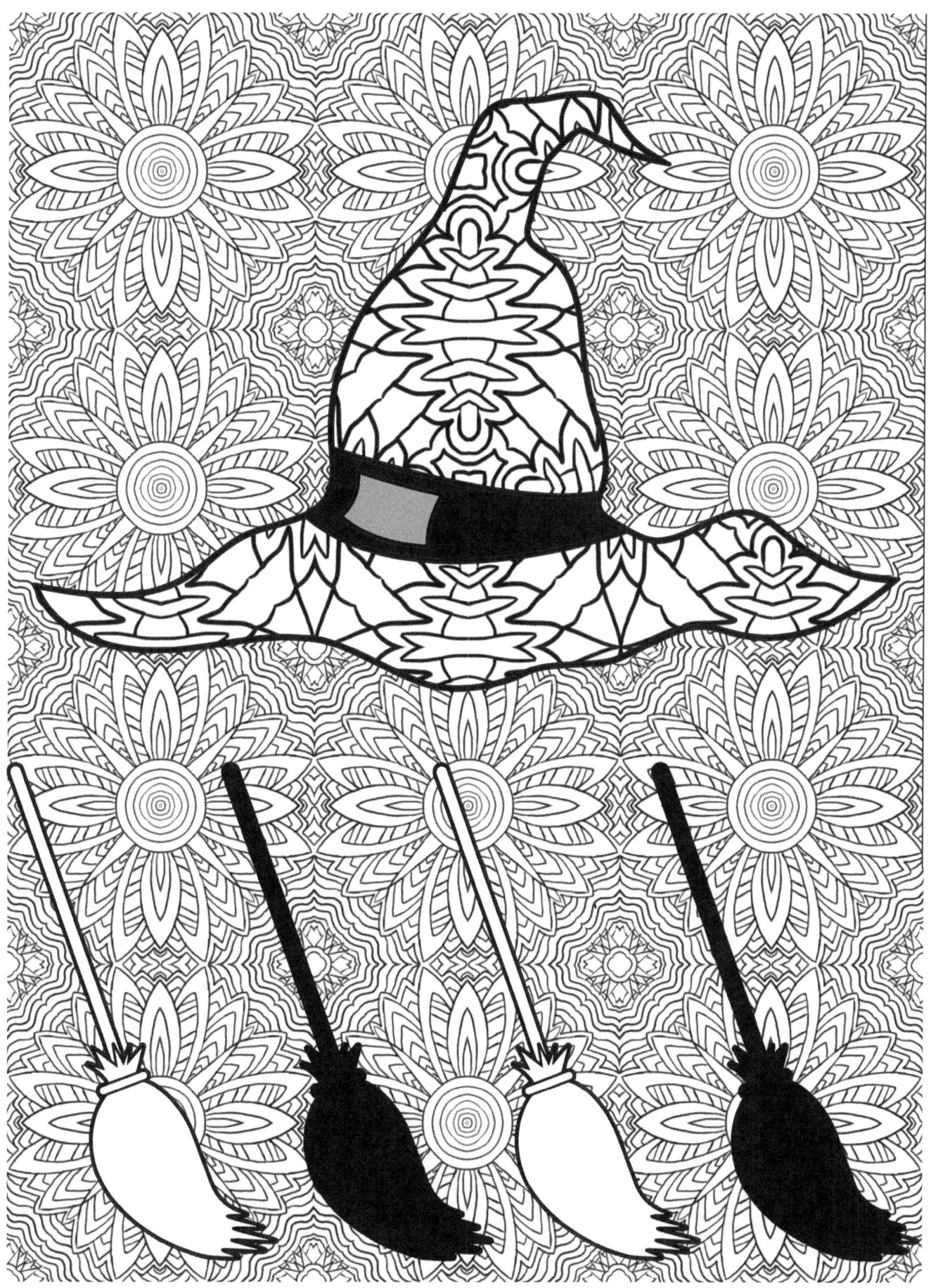

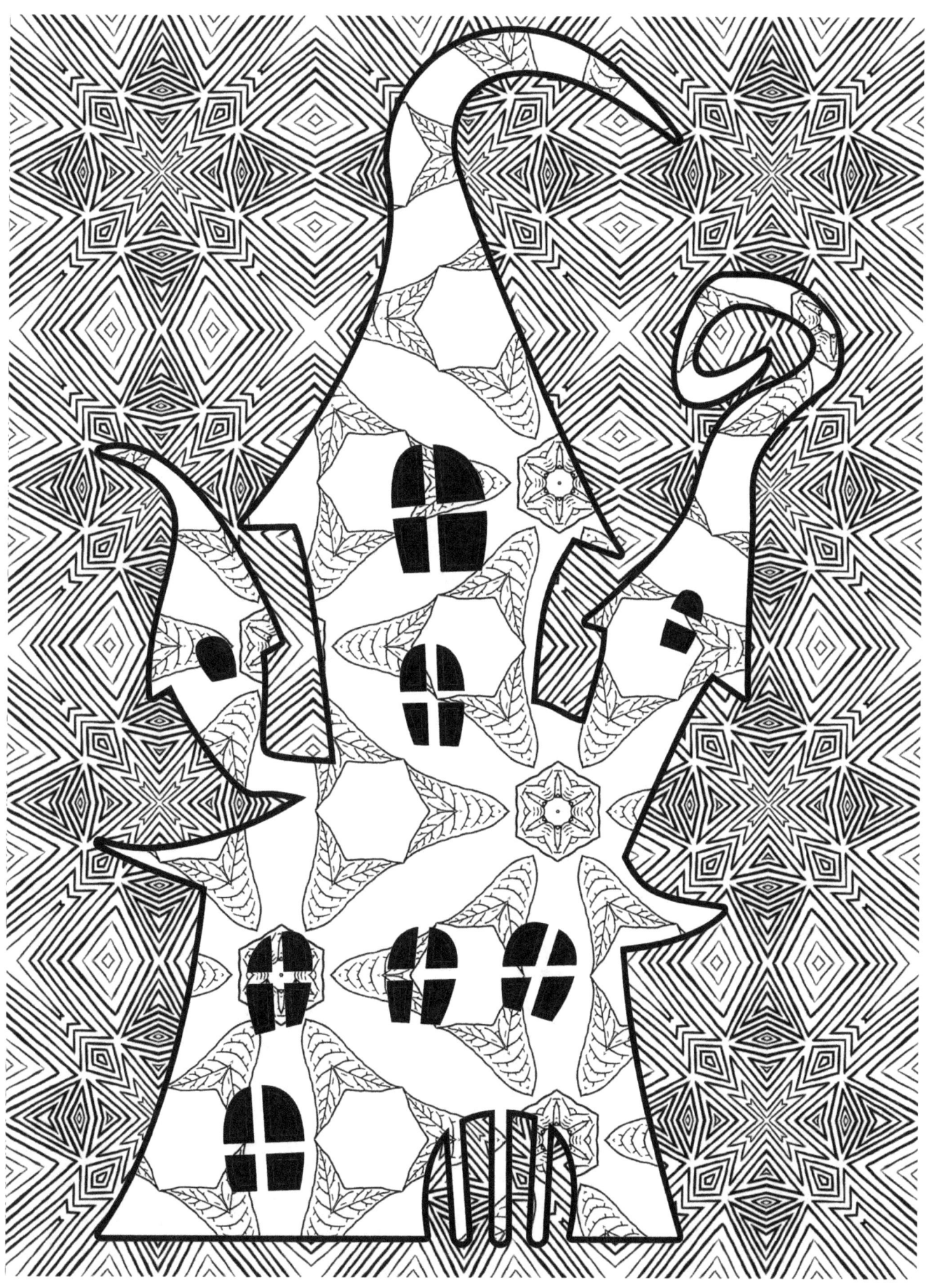

ABOUT THE ILLUSTRATOR

Kimberly Eldredge is a third generation Arizona native. She graduated from the University of Arizona with a degree in Creative Writing. She has been writing all her life and has been published in poetry journals, short story anthologies, and regional travel magazines.

In addition to loving patterns and coloring, Kimberly also writes a blog at NewFrontierBooks.com with topics including writing, editing, and publishing.

She is also fluent in Spanish and has written several children's stories in Spanish.

Kimberly lives in Chino Valley, Arizona, with her husband, Ben, and son, Connor.

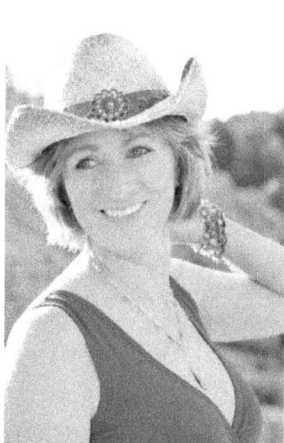

Other Books Available From Kimberly Eldredge

Adult Coloring Books:
Symmetry Art: An Adult Coloring Book
ISBN-13: 978-1519402547

Symmetry Art: An Adult Coloring Book - 30 New Designs of Radial Symmetry
ISBN-13: 978-1519642738

Other Titles:
Scary & Silly Campfire Stories: Fifteen Tales For Shivers & Giggles (Volume 1)
ISBN: 978-0615690902

Scary & Silly Campfire Stories: Fifteen Spooky & Silly Tales (Volume 2)
ISBN: 978-0615701165

Scary & Silly Campfire Stories: Fifteen Scary & Silly Stories (Volume 3)
ISBN: 978-0615741130

Pitch Your Tent: A Family's Guide To Tent Camping
ISBN: 978-1492857761

Camp Cooking 101:
101 Fun & Easy Recipes from The Outdoor Princess
ISBN: 978-1492120476

My Camping Recipes: A Personal Collection
(A blank book to fill with your favorite camping recipes)
ISBN: 978-1492191261

www.ingramcontent.com/pod-product-compliance
Lightning Source LLC
Chambersburg PA
CBHW082359220526
45470CB00008B/2805